# Meat Pies and Mumbling Blokes

Also by Margitta Acker
*Vom Ostseestrand in fernes Land* (Zeitgut Verlag, Berlin, 2008)

Margitta Acker

# Meat Pies and Mumbling Blokes

## Acknowledgements

A sincere thank you to Judy for pointing out my inconsistencies, to Sylvia for showing me the way, to Stephen for taking me on board and, most of all, to Chris for his unwavering support, his patience and understanding.

*Meat Pies and Mumbling Blokes*
ISBN 978 1 74027 833 1
Copyright © Margitta Acker 2013

First published 2013
Reprinted 2014, 2015

GINNINDERRA PRESS
PO Box 3461 Port Adelaide 5015
www.ginninderrapress.com.au

# Contents

| | | |
|---|---|---|
| 1 | Arriving – meat pies and mumbling blokes | 7 |
| 2 | The wedding – alone among strangers | 22 |
| 3 | Settling in – guineas and swear words | 34 |
| 4 | Fishing and other adventures in the bush | 51 |
| 5 | Working – typewriters and tea ladies | 62 |
| 6 | A home of our own – bare walls and bare earth | 72 |
| 7 | And then we were four – nappies flapping in the wind | 84 |
| 8 | Everyday life – lamingtons and lingerie | 99 |
| 9 | Going home – $800 and thirty-six hours one way | 108 |
| 10 | Visitors – a welcome on the tarmac | 119 |
| 11 | The years fly past – a citizen at last | 128 |
| 12 | Belonging | 137 |

# 1

# Arriving – meat pies and mumbling blokes

On 22 June 1962 I first set foot on Australian soil. It was in Fremantle. I had come to Australia to be married.

Fremantle harbour in those days, all those decades ago, was nothing like it is today. Impersonal, it looked forlorn, desolate even, and a bit grubby. It was winter; the sky was grey and heavy with cloud as our vessel slowly entered the harbour. None of that fabled Australian sunshine anywhere. But never mind a bit of disappointment. We were all eager to have a first curious look at this place. After four weeks at sea, we were ready for solid ground.

We – my fellow travellers and I – had come to this country, this continent, for a variety of reasons: to get to know the big wide world, to get away from tired Europe, to start a new life, to find riches perhaps or, like me, to be married. In Fremantle we took our first tentative steps on this vast continent many of us would come to call home, breathed the cool and salty air of this faraway land, felt the wind in our hair and looked about us full of curiosity. What was it going to be like, our life in Australia? How defining would first impressions be? Would they set the tone for all there was to come? Or would they mean nothing at all?

A month earlier we had embarked on the *Fairsea* at Bremerhaven, Germany. I had arrived there two days earlier and was being accommodated in a migrant hostel. Being a country girl and a potential agricultural disease carrier, I had to be disinfected: that is, not only did the contents of my luggage – and I was carrying quite a bit – have to be sprayed, I had to submit to a thorough, disinfecting shower. The disinfectant may have been DDT, but I do not know.

My luggage consisted of a large wooden crate that our village carpenter had made for me. It contained my dowry: a twelve-piece dinner set, off-white and gold-rimmed, complete with serving dishes, a soup tureen, a saucier and meat platters, as well as a dozen cups and saucers, a teapot and a coffee pot. And then there was the cutlery: knives, forks, spoons, teaspoons, cake forks, soup ladles, sauce ladles, cake server and so on; all in silver – supposedly to be polished on a regular basis. The crate also contained bath towels and tea towels and some bed linen, but not much, as I had been told Australian beds and bedding were different from the German variety. The spaces between the crate's 'hardware' were filled with pretty little things like tea cosies, egg warmers and doilies I had stitched, embroidered or embellished during the months of waiting for a passage to Australia. This crate also contained a dainty and beautifully decorated Japanese tea set for six that my fiancé had wanted me to obtain in Germany. I couldn't see why he would want something so delicate. Would we ever use it?

Apart from this crate, there was a smaller one containing a large Grundig radio which had been packed at the factory. As cabin luggage I had a brand-new suitcase and a rather battered kitbag. These contained my personal belongings, among them a couple of treasured books and a stack of airmail letters, some forty or fifty in all, which my fiancé had written to me since we had parted in Germany some fourteen months earlier.

Three weeks before my departure, my parents had moved farms. From being a farm manager, my father had become the lessee of a combined farm and country pub. It was a major event in the life of our family. I had helped as much as I could with the move, but foremost in my mind had always been my own much more substantial move – or so it seemed to me – to the other side of the globe. Things at home had been frantic, and I think my parents were relieved when I told them that I did not expect anyone to accompany me to Bremerhaven, that I was quite happy to go on my own, to take the train. The crate had already left for Bremerhaven a week or so earlier. What I really wanted to avoid was a tearful farewell, a farewell that would have been much more poignant, much more heart-jerking on a migrant vessel in a busy port than at a small country railway station.

At the migrant hostel, soon after I had come out of the disinfecting shower, I met Rosemarie from Cologne, who was going to Australia simply for the fun of it; Rudi, her boyfriend, was coming along. Then other young people turned up, mostly single, a few young married couples, even fewer families.

Early the next day, buses took us to the quay. We walked up the gangway – some quickly as if they couldn't wait, others more slowly, more thoughtfully. Were they having second thoughts?

We found our cabins, deposited our luggage and went out on deck. Soon the big vessel was gliding down the mouth of the Weser River towards the open sea, the North Sea. Farewell songs boomed across the water from the pilot station: *Muss i' denn, muss i' denn, zum Städele hinaus* (a German farewell folk song) and another catchy, but as yet unknown, tune which would be played again once we arrived at the other end as well as at every port of call along the way, 'Waltzing Matilda'.

Did I cry? I don't think so, even if my heart was heavy, which surely it must have been. I wanted to be brave and not get carried away by my emotions. Rosemarie and her boyfriend were standing next to me at the railing as we listened to the music and hummed along, our eyes firmly fixed on the horizon ahead of us.

Here we were on a sparkling white ship on sparkling blue seas. Wonderful! The voyage had initially been exhilarating: six young women to a cabin, we all felt as if we were on an ocean cruise and not on a migrant ship. The words 'migrant ship' seemed to carry the connotation of something basic, crowded and somehow ugly. But this was bliss: beautiful meals, certainly meals more glamorous than I'd ever had in my life; swimming pools, deck chairs for sunbaking, entertainment every evening, from movies and games to dances, an equatorial baptism, a fancy dress ball at which – so my diary tells me – the captain asked me for a dance, not once, but twice. And yet I have no recollection of that. All of this – apart from a small administrative fee – came with the compliments of the Australian government. Because of my status as an assisted nominated dependent, who had been sponsored by her future husband, I was wanted in Australia.

Our first port of call where more migrants joined us was Southampton. Then, after the stormy Bay of Biscay, we took on board a small number of Spanish migrants at Vigo on the north-western tip of Spain. We rounded Gibraltar and left the cool and blustery Atlantic for the more placid Mediterranean. We docked at Naples, and migrants from Italy and the then Yugoslavia came on board; then at Piraeus Greek migrants joined us. They and most of the Italians were accommodated in a separate part of the vessel and took their meals at a different sitting to ours. With few exceptions and then only among young people, the migrants from northern Europe did not mix with the migrants from southern ports.

After Piraeus, the *Fairsea* had its full complement of passengers. Now it was full steam ahead for Australia. Or so we thought. But then there was the Suez Canal to negotiate. There was Port Said at the northern end of the canal, where hawkers and traders bombarded us with their exotic merchandise: leatherware, copperware, knick-knacks. For very little money, I acquired a pair of rubber thongs. I had never seen, let alone owned, something as exotic as these and sent my parents a postcard from our next port, Aden, describing my purchase and drawing a sketch of them.

Aden, at the southern end of the Red Sea, was only the second port on this voyage where we were allowed to go on land, Naples having been the other. How much I had also wanted to wander the streets of the other ports! Now we – my cabin friends, a married couple, some young men – were wandering through the streets of Aden, then a British crown colony. While Naples and Piraeus had still had an air of familiarity about them, Aden was another world: hot, dusty, crowded, noisy, alien. Goats roamed the sandy streets, men in what looked to us like rags were sitting about. Smells. We soon fled to the safety of the vessel.

After Aden there was the Indian Ocean, interminably long, vast, never-ending, monotonous, boring. No more ports of call, only the towering sky, drifting clouds, and water whichever way one looked. Sleek dolphins and large schools of tiny silvery fish that seemed to fly across the waves accompanied us from time to time. The exhilaration of the early days eventually vanished. The voyage was dragging on. I couldn't wait for it to end, even though my anxiety levels were increasing as the distance to Australia decreased.

On 22 June, we were up early, everyone wanting to be first to spot a sliver of Australia on the eastern horizon. Standing at the railing with my shipboard friends, I watched that sliver of land gradually grow more substantial, eventually making out an island, buildings, beaches, port facilities. Fremantle. We watched while the vessel docked and then gingerly walked down the gangway. Finally we stood on solid ground, still swaying slightly after a month of rolling seas.

Australia! Here we were at last, although for most of the passengers the final destination was not isolated Western Australia but the much better known cities of Melbourne and Sydney, another four to six days on the water, weathering the infamous storms of the Great Australian Bight. I was prone to seasickness and during the voyage had occasionally suffered an upset of the internal system. I was not looking forward to crossing the Bight. But I was being spared. The day before we docked at Fremantle, the ship's purser had advised me that I would be disembarking and flying east instead. A gentleman from the bank (the Commonwealth?) had come aboard that morning with all necessary documentation and explained how I was to proceed. My fiancé had organised an airline ticket for me. I would be taking the TAA flight to Melbourne at midnight. What a relief! My crates, meanwhile, would travel on to Sydney alone; my suitcase and kitbag would come with me now. Why Melbourne, I wondered, as my original final destination was to be Sydney. No one could tell me, but I was assured that I would be met at Melbourne airport.

But first it was time to look at Fremantle, to see what an Australian town looked like. And we looked with curious, but also rather critical, European eyes. The few shops we came across with their meagre window displays were of little interest. We looked for a café where we could sit down, preferably outside like in Europe, and have a cup of coffee and a piece of cake. We could find no outside eating areas. Was it because it was winter? Surely outdoor cafés would not be unknown here? All we managed to find were milk bars selling soft drinks, gaudily coloured ice creams, meat pies (what on earth were they?), tea with milk and some dark brew that went under the name of coffee. I later found out that some of this so-called coffee came out of a tube and wasn't real coffee at all. Nonetheless, we entered and sat down on vinyl-covered chairs at a laminated metal table; and the coffee drinkers among us shuddered at the coffee that was being served.

There was little traffic on the streets, and the vehicles all seemed to be of pre-war vintage, imported from England, and not a VW in sight. Most of us had gone very quiet. Was this what the whole country was like, so drab, so old-fashioned? Surely Sydney and Melbourne would not be like this? Perhaps Fremantle was an exception because of its remoteness and because it was a port town?

But then we suddenly all burst out laughing. We noticed a small, rather dilapidated truck in the street. It did not have indicators, just a metal arm instead, which, when the driver pushed a lever, went out to indicate that a right-hand turn was desired. Had the truck driver wanted to turn left, the mechanical arm would have pointed downward, and had he wanted to stop, the arm would have pointed upwards. Many truck and car drivers used their own arms in the same fashion, even though ordinary cars did have proper indicators, although not yet of the flashing kind.

We had spent our first Australian money, exchanged on board ship, at the milk bar on a drink of some sort. Most of us did not carry much money, or at least were very careful about spending it. On board ship we'd had the occasional drink at the bar – Singapore sling was my favourite. Didn't I feel ever so worldly, sitting on a bar stool sucking on a straw and slowly imbibing this exotic and alluring drink! Apart from the bar there had been little opportunity during the voyage to spend money, with the exception perhaps of Port Said.

Eventually our wander through Fremantle came to an end, and it was time to say goodbye and for my friends to return to the *Fairsea*. Soon we were back at the quay and everyone walked up the gangway – everyone except me. I stayed behind. Alone. I don't recall our goodbyes. Did we hug? Did we shake hands as was the German tradition? Rosemarie, Rudi, the others with whom I had shared a cabin or a table at mealtimes and whose names I have long since forgotten, all went back on board ship.

I watched my friends as they climbed the gangway and leant over the railing far above me. We shouted final messages, looked away, looked again. It seemed to take an awfully long time for the gangway to be pulled up and for the ship to get moving, but eventually it did pull away ever so slowly from the quay, a blast announcing its imminent departure. My friends waved, with handkerchiefs, with jackets, and I waved back wondering if I would ever see them again. Slowly the vessel turned and headed for the open sea. Away into the sunset it headed, and I stood, lonely and as alone as I have ever been in my life, by the water's edge still facing west, with a vast continent behind me, so immeasurably vast and so totally unknown. My parents, my siblings, my school friends – they were thousands of miles away; and my new-found friends, my fellow migrants, were disappearing over the horizon. It felt unreal. I wondered whether in fact I wasn't dreaming. Was I really standing at the edge of a continent on the other side of the globe?

One last look at the horizon where the *Fairsea* was disappearing into the sunset, and then I resolutely turned around. There was no point in dwelling on my sadness and my loneliness. I was facing east now, facing the future. Tonight I would fly across this continent to meet someone several thousand miles away whom I had not seen for many, many months. Had I not had a passport photo of him to look at once in a while to refresh my memory, I would barely have remembered what he looked like. Yet, before long I was going to marry this man. The voyage had been an interlude. Now a new phase in my life was about to begin. There were things to be done.

As instructed in my travel advice, I boarded a bus for Perth. Daylight was fading, but I could still make out enough details of the suburbs through which the bus was travelling. The streets were wide with lots of green either as open spaces or parks, and palm trees were swaying in the evening breeze. Square, squat little houses of timber or stone lined the streets, their red metal roofs extending over the front veranda; heavy curtains inside small windows excluded the outside world; small patches of grass, perhaps a shrub or two, rarely a flower (I kept forgetting that it was winter here), made up the front gardens which were bordered by a low hedge or a picket fence. The word cute came to mind, yet in their squatness, the houses also looked withdrawn, as if they were afraid of the wind and the world.

The TAA office in Perth was anything but glamorous. I checked in, but as my flight was not until midnight, I had a four-hour wait ahead of me. Fortunately, there was a comfortable chair and I had a book to keep my mind occupied and any doubts at bay. But the doubts kept intruding. What if it did not work out? What if the man I fell in love with at a wine festival more than two years ago had changed and was no longer as I remembered him? What if I didn't like it in Australia? What if I got homesick? The answer to all these what-ifs was that I was here for a minimum of two years, that was my agreement with the Australian government, for that I had free passage. If it really did not work out, I could go back. And so my thoughts went round and round. I was terribly tired, too. My shipmates and I had partied the last two nights and got up early that morning. All I wanted to do was sleep and bury my concerns.

By the time the TAA bus took me and a few other passengers to Perth airport, I wished for nothing more than sleep. I remember little of the flight, whether there was a meal or whether I slept; all I remember is dragging myself out of my seat for the stopover at

Adelaide. It was early morning; outside it was cold and grey. Soon we were airborne again, rising above the clouds. The sun was coming up in the east. The cloudscape was magic: a vast expanse of fluffy white as far as the eye could see. Like snow on the moon, I thought. I had never seen anything like it before. Then, suddenly, there was an opening in the fluffy white carpet to reveal a green and fertile countryside below crisscrossed by roads and the occasional settlement. Then more houses and before I knew it the plane touched down at Melbourne (Essendon) airport. I had arrived, I thought, and my heart began to beat faster. I followed the other passengers to the terminal building and soon found myself in the arrivals lounge.

I took the passport photo out of my handbag, looked at it again and scanned the faces of the men who stood there waiting. No one looked in the least familiar. Perhaps someone other than my fiancé would meet me? There was no way I would recognise him, but hopefully he would recognise me. Then I heard my name being called over the public address system. At the information counter there was a phone call for me. But it wasn't my fiancé; it was his boss, advising me that due to heavy fog on the highway, there had been traffic delays and he, my fiancé, would be about thirty minutes late. More waiting, but at least the right person was coming for me.

Patiently I waited for the next half hour. Then I became restless again. I strode back and forth through the hall, peering at faces, searching for the one familiar one, but could not find it. I went outside, wandered up and down there, too, scrutinising every arriving car for that particular face. Half an hour had long passed. I went back into the hall, came out again.

An hour must have passed when finally, finally, a familiar figure emerged from between the parked cars. It was him. At long last it was him. I had no trouble recognising him. And as we hugged, the doubts just flew away.

In my application for migration I had indicated that I would prefer to go to Australia by air rather than by sea. But that did not eventuate.

As I found out many years later from records at the National Archives of Australia, flying to the other side of the globe was not an option for me because of my rural background and the possibility, however remote, of importing diseases unknown to farmers here. With hindsight I must say that, more than anything, those many weeks at sea really brought home the realisation of the distance that now lay between what I had known all my life and the new life I was about to begin. Sitting in an airplane for twenty-four, thirty-six or even forty-eight hours would simply not have conveyed that same message.

A colleague had lent Chris, my fiancé, his car, a green VW (oh, there were VWs on this side of the continent at least!) and he had been given a week off work. At the time he was working for a Sydney-based telecommunications company that was connecting all telephone exchanges between Sydney and Melbourne to the newly installed coaxial cable. Currently they were working at Seymour, and the drive to Melbourne that morning had been hampered not only by a combination of thick fog and heavy traffic, but also because the telegram announcing my arrival had reached Chris only forty-five minutes before my plane was due to touch down in Melbourne. But now all was well.

Memories of the two days we spent in Melbourne are vague and blurry. I remember seeing some high-rise buildings from our motel room. We had checked into the Parkroyal Motel in the city as Mr and Mrs Acker – rather daring, we felt, because only married couples were allowed to stay in a double room. This was 1962, after all. Fortunately, no identification was required of me, only of Chris. I had never stayed in a hotel or motel before, only in youth hostel dormitories. So the room at the Parkroyal with en suite and television made quite an impression on me. But more than anything, I wanted to sleep. Melbourne could wait, and my patient fiancé had no choice either.

Exploring the city and its surrounds did not happen until the next day. We strolled through the city and later went to the Botanic Gardens, to the shores of Port Phillip Bay and the St Kilda pier. However, it wasn't the city so much that I wanted to see as the countryside. So the next day, we left Melbourne and drove to the wildlife sanctuary at Healesville in the Dandenong Ranges to satisfy one of my curiosities about Australia – to see a kangaroo.

While our first day in Melbourne had been rather dull and grey, when we set off for Healesville the sun was shining. At the sanctuary I not only made the acquaintance of kangaroos, I also fed emus, admired koalas and listened to the cheerful garble of magpies and the ear-piercing cackle of kookaburras – a name that rolled off the tongue rather harshly. The wildlife park was devoid of people as it was winter and mid-week. Not that we needed people; I was far too absorbed with these strange-looking animals and, once we had seen them, I guess we were much too absorbed with each other. Apart from the animals, what also immediately appealed were the cool forests of towering eucalyptus trees and the shady fern-filled gullies. So different to the beech and oak forests of my home country, different and beautiful.

On my third day in Australia, we drove to Seymour, where I met some of Chris's colleagues and, for the first time in my life, I got to sit inside a caravan sipping a cup of tea. White tea. Very English! In Germany, I would have been offered a cup of coffee and probably a piece of cake. But this was a man's world and tea was what everyone in this country drank, I realised. The technicians lived in the caravans and, as they moved from town to town, their homes moved right along with them. This was also my first glimpse of a caravan park, but I remember nothing of it – in later years, caravan parks and campgrounds were to become an important feature of our lives.

The Germans thrive on handshakes, the stronger the grip the better. A lame handshake is supposedly a sign of a lame character; a moist, lame handshake even worse. So they used to say! Here only men shook hands with each other, a man and a woman did not. One just nodded and smiled at the other. That was the proper way of greeting in this country, I was told. Or at least it was the proper way then. There was no woman around for me to find out how women greeted each other, and I forgot to ask. Introductions were on a first-name basis only. This was Bob, this was John and so on. In Germany it would have been much more formal – definitely no first names.

Another thing that surprised me: I had trouble understanding the Australians and their English. I had had a thorough grounding in the English language and considered myself reasonably fluent in it. I knew the grammar, I could spell, but could I understand these Australian blokes? No. And blokes for one was a word I had never heard before; and even less had I ever heard of sheilas, the blokes' companions, as it was explained to me. These men here, Chris's colleagues, all spoke fast in some, to me, unfamiliar jargon and all of them seemed to talk through clenched teeth barely moving their lips, except for one man: Gabor, a Hungarian migrant who spoke loudly and with a pronounced accent. I did not understand him either. I often looked to Chris for help in understanding what the blokes were asking or commenting on. I was rather embarrassed by it all.

Equally embarrassing for me was the fact that I was expected to speak to Chris in English in front of these men. I had been told – and it made a great deal of sense to me – that it was considered very impolite to speak a language other than English in front of people who knew no other language than English. It took a while – Perhaps a year? Maybe even longer – before I felt comfortable talking to Chris in English in front of others.

From Seymour we drove to Albury and, once we had checked into a motel, again as Mr and Mrs, we drove to Bonegilla to have a look at its migrant hostel where some of my friends from the *Fairsea* would soon be arriving. Bonegilla did not look like a very inviting place, and I was glad I was being spared the migrant hostel experience. We continued on to the mighty Hume Weir and drove along its shores. The many dead trees sticking out of the water were indeed a ghostly sight.

Our motel in Albury was not quite as posh as the one in Melbourne. Just like caravan parks, motels were a novelty for me. My family in Germany had never gone on a holiday, and on the few occasions we had gone away it had been to visit relatives and stay with them. There certainly was a pub in our village with a few guest rooms and the nearest town had a hotel; but motels – these rows of rooms with a car parking space in front of each – were virtually unknown in Germany at that time. The oddest thing about the motels for me was the way guests were served their breakfast. It was ordered the night before by ticking relevant boxes on a menu and indicating the preferred time for delivery. The menu was then left at reception. The next morning, at the requested time, there was a knock on the door and a hatch next to it would open and a tray or trays laden with food would slide in as if by magic. The occupant of the room would shout a 'thank you', and a mumbled 'you're welcome' from an unseen source was the usual reply.

After Albury our next destination was Canberra, although we detoured via Wagga Wagga. What a strange name! And why were we going to Canberra? For the time being, Chris's work would be taking place somewhere, anywhere, between Sydney and Melbourne. It made more sense to place me in between those two cities rather than at either end; and the reason Chris favoured Canberra over, for example, Albury, was that he had friends there. These friends had offered to take me in until we had found a place of our own. So, on 26 June 1962, a Sunday, we headed for Australia's capital. I had only recently heard of Canberra; I had thought that either Sydney or Melbourne was the country's capital. In fact, I had to admit to myself that I knew very little about this continent that was supposed to become my home. I knew the seasons were opposite to those of the northern hemisphere. I had heard of Captain Cook and his voyages of discovery and through some strange coincidence I had heard of Cooma and the Snowy Mountains scheme, but had no idea how close they were to Canberra.

It was a rather grey winter's day, with the sun peeking through the clouds only occasionally, as we drove along the then narrow and winding Hume Highway, through an undulating landscape with the occasional village or small town, past vast fields and paddocks full of sheep. Yes, that was another thing I knew about Australia: there were lots of sheep and the wool was exported to England for processing.

And then there were the gum trees, the ones that stood alone or in small clusters by the side of the road, in the middle of a paddock or on a small rise. I didn't know they were called gum trees. To me they were eucalyptus trees. I had never seen such wily trees before. No beautifully shaped evenly rounded crown sitting on top of a straight and sturdy trunk like the oaks and beech trees I knew. No, these trees looked wild and free and wilful. They had that couldn't-care-less-what-you-think attitude. I didn't realise it then, nor did I for a long time, that that was precisely why I came to like them so much over the years, not for their cough-lolly fragrance nor for their gentle dappled shade, but for their unruliness, their undisciplined look, their messiness. But in 1962, to me, gum trees just messed up the countryside.

How empty was the country we had travelled through. Fifty, eighty, a hundred miles (no kilometres then) between settlements seemed to be nothing unusual. In contrast, on a German highway, in a hundred miles one would have gone through several small towns and passed a few villages. Here, somewhere off the highway we occasionally spotted a farm, its buildings looking rather unimpressive. While the farmhouse itself was often hidden behind a hedge or under some tall trees, the other farm buildings were nothing more than an assembly of tentative structures of mostly corrugated iron with a sprinkling of machinery, new or rusted, in between. Were these farmers here poor? Could they not afford to build a decent barn? A decent brick shed for their tractor? It certainly looked like that.

Not only did most farms have a neglected look about them, the small towns through which we passed often looked equally uninspiring; a bit like in the wild west, I thought, when I looked at the shopfronts and the corner pub. Outside the towns and villages, the roadsides too had an unkempt look, with beer bottles, an occasional car or truck tyre, and paper lying about. And the messy gum trees didn't help either.

Later that day, we passed through Yass, not much more than a village. Then our little green VW beetle turned south, the countryside still unchanged. Yet gradually, mountains, not just hills, began to appear on the horizon. The Dandenong Ranges had been a first surprise; I had imagined Australia to be a flat country of mostly desert with a few hills perhaps along the coastal strip. And here now real mountains covered in forests were rising up on the western horizon and wooded hills dotted the landscape closer to town. I come from the flat country of Germany's north and to me mountains have always held an air of mystery and allure.

Chris's friends, Max and Gerda, lived in Lyneham, then on Canberra's northern fringe. In 1955 Chris and Max had become friends when they came to Australia on the same migrant ship. They had subsequently lost contact and then miraculously rediscovered each other at a German club function in Geelong in Victoria a few years later. Chris was living in Geelong at the time, and Max was passing through with his wife. They had recently married and were spending their honeymoon cruising around the country, or at least a small part of it. Their home, however, was in Canberra, where Max had found work and where Gerda had come from Germany with her parents.

Now, as we were about to turn up on their doorstep, they were living with their two young children, Henry and Mark, in a semi-detached two-storey house. Initially, after their honeymoon, they had lived in the converted garage at Gerda's parents' house down the street. Before their second child was born, and after a three-year wait, they had been allocated a government house and were happy at last to be in their own home. They had already paid a deposit on it and intended to pay off the loan as soon as they could. Semi-detached houses were generally not as popular as free-standing ones but years later, when town houses became fashionable, semi-detached homes easily fell into that category. Here, in Max and Gerda's house, kitchen, living and dining areas were downstairs, three bedrooms upstairs: one for the parents, one for the boys, the third a spare. Did we sleep together, Gerda wanted to know, or would we rather be in separate rooms? I am not sure where she would have put one of us had we preferred separateness. We got the spare bedroom. And that was where I stayed until our wedding day.

# 2

# The wedding – alone among strangers

Two tasks were now of utmost importance: to arrange our wedding and to find a place to live; and those two tasks had to go hand in hand, because, at the time, couples could only rent a house or a flat or a room if they were married, or so at least it was said. We did not put it to the test.

Max had already been on the lookout for suitable accommodation for us. There was very little available. Canberra was a busy place: public servants were being moved there; construction workers were filling the hostels; building activity could not keep up with demand. Max knew a German builder who had just finished his own home in Holmes Crescent, Campbell, and was prepared to fit out a room on the lower ground floor at the back of the house if we were prepared to advance the funds. Which we were. We met the builder and checked out the space: the total living area was no bigger than a single-car garage. But it would do for a start. It had to do. Details of the fit-out were discussed: shelving in the kitchen, a sink and a stove, a wardrobe as a divider between kitchen and living/sleeping area, a tiny fold-down table for meals. Shower and toilet were across the small entrance area; the laundry would be shared with the owners. Expected date of completion: mid to late July. Our wedding date was set for 28 July.

But first of all we had to go to Sydney. The *Fairsea* was due soon, and we had to collect my crates – my dowry and our wireless. As shopping options in Canberra were limited, we took a long shopping list with us: we needed a sofa bed, two easy chairs, a coffee table and two kitchen stools. We also needed a number of kitchen gadgets, pots and pans, some everyday crockery and cutlery. My twelve-piece dinner set and silver cutlery were not really meant for everyday use and with the limited cupboard space in the bedsitter, they would remain in the crate for the time being. Chris already owned an electric frypan and a Sunbeam toaster. The latter, believe it or not, is still in use after fifty years.

Actually, the most important item on our shopping list was my wedding dress. Unlike some migrant brides-to-be, I had not brought one with me. Gerda suggested I should have it made in Sydney; she even gave us the address of a bridal shop, and that was where we went. In my romantic moments I used to dream of a church wedding in spring when the world was full of flowers and fragrances. But July was deepest winter in Canberra. A long-sleeved dress seemed appropriate, but I did not want a long dress – short wedding dresses had just become the fashion in Germany. The material we chose was pale eggshell satin; the veil would be short, the dress basically plain with some lacy embellishments around the neckline. Chris needed a new suit. Ordering all this proved relatively easy. It took much longer to find the right style and colour of furniture that would be ready and delivered to Canberra before the end of July. Even in Sydney choices seemed limited.

On the appointed day we went to the international terminal at Circular Quay where the *Fairsea* had arrived that morning. Customs clearance of my crates proceeded smoothly. Afterwards we met Rosemarie and spent some time with her. All my other shipboard companions had disembarked in Melbourne; most had gone to the Bonegilla migrant hostel. Rosemarie had been offered a job as a maid with a wealthy widow in Sydney's eastern suburbs. She was a trained bookkeeper but could not work as such because of her limited English. In those days, most migrants – whether skilled or not, whether English-literate or not – tended to start their Australian working lives in manual jobs: in factories, as domestics, with the railways, or picking fruit.

On this first visit to Sydney, of course we made some time for sightseeing. While Chris called in to his company headquarters, I took the lift to the top of the AMP building at Circular Quay, then the city's tallest building, and gazed down at the expansive harbour and the wooded shores opposite, and later took a long walk through the Botanic Gardens. This was exciting stuff for a country girl. Up till now, ever since landing in Fremantle, I seemed to have walked around in some sort of fuzzy daze; it suddenly dawned on me here in Sydney, at the top of the AMP building, that I really was in Australia, at the far end of the globe, the other side of the world, and that I was going to be married in a few weeks' time. I felt a mixture of thrill, trepidation and anxiety.

After three days we returned to Canberra. There was no freeway between Sydney and Canberra then. The Hume Highway wound its tortuous way through small towns and tiny villages, uphill and downhill, through sharp bends and along some straight and boring stretches, always just two lanes and many double yellow lines. It was slow going, particularly when one got stuck behind a truck going up Razorback Mountain near Picton. And before long we would have to do the trip again in order to pick up my wedding dress and Chris's suit.

The eye catcher on the trip between Canberra and Sydney was Lake George, that vast body of water that looked a bit like an inland sea; at least it did then. Before Canberra had its own lake, watersport-keen Canberrans used to go there to sail their boats or try and catch a fish on sometimes choppy and dangerous waters. There was a myth about this lake. No one knew exactly where its waters came from or where they went to, as no river flowed into it or out of it. Perhaps there was an unknown water source somewhere deep down, I was told; perhaps some mysterious underground opening went all the way to New Zealand. No one knew, but everyone seemed to have an opinion. Some years later, during a fairly wet winter or spring, the lake rose to such a level that the highway was under water and had to be closed and the Sydney–Canberra detour went via Yass. After that, the water level of the lake gradually receded, and at some stage the lake disappeared altogether and the farmers had their paddocks back.

Back in Canberra, I stayed with Max and Gerda while Chris returned to work, down the Hume Highway, to Seymour perhaps or detouring to Wagga Wagga or some other small town, always to return on Friday night. There were many things that needed attention, and Gerda proved an invaluable source of support and information. She was only a few months older than I, but she was married, a mother of two who had lived in Canberra for a number of years. She knew her way around. We discussed and tossed ideas around about the wedding: the invitations, the venue for the ceremony and the reception, the flowers – all those details that are more easily and best sorted out between women. Then on Friday night, Chris was presented with the options.

We were going to be married in the recently completed St Peter's Lutheran Church in Reid, the A-frame building with the once green roof. Chris would have been happy with a civil wedding but he relented, seeing how much a church wedding meant to me. Pastor Röhrs, moreover, spoke German and suggested we do the vows in both English and German.

Our wedding thus became a melding of German and Australian traditions. I would walk down the aisle on Chris's arm – that was how it was done at home: bride and groom walked down the aisle together. In any case, there was no father to give me away and the only other familiar male, Max, was a bit too young for that. Our engagement rings were plain gold bands, engraved on the inside with each other's names. In the German tradition, the rings were worn on the left hand during the time of the engagement. At the wedding those same rings were changed over to the right hand. But here, a wedding ring belonged on the left hand. So at our wedding, we would simply take the rings off beforehand; and they would be returned to the same place on the left hand at the ceremony. For the wedding reception we had booked a room at the Ainslie Hotel (now Olim's Mercure), one of only a few places in Canberra where dinner dances were held on Saturday nights.

Who to invite? Apart from Max and Gerda the only other person I knew in Australia and whose address I had was Rosemarie. Chris had some friends in Geelong, where he had lived for five years before he returned to Germany for a visit in 1960 – that fateful visit when our paths crossed. He doubted that any of them would undertake the seven-hundred-kilometre trip to be at the wedding. As it turned out, he was right. That left his colleagues and their wives or girlfriends as well as a couple – Ian and Roma from Geelong – whom Chris had befriended on his 1960 voyage to Germany and who were now living in Canberra, Ian a teacher at Canberra Boys' Grammar School. The invitations were printed to the customary formula, and we also had some printed in German, not invitations as such, more like an announcement, because we wanted to let our relatives and friends in Germany know of our wedding plans.

Shortly after mid-July it was back to Sydney. This time we left Friday afternoon and returned on Sunday. We collected our wedding wear and all was satisfactory. Then Chris had a surprise for me: he bought me a diamond ring, so that after 28 July my ringed left hand would look the same as that of any other married Australian woman. It is still there today. He also bought me a pearl necklace to go with my wedding dress.

We dropped in to our little bedsitter once or twice to check on progress. All was proceeding to plan. When the crates arrived, we unpacked the one with the radio; and a local cabinetmaker (German, of course) made a special cabinet for it, with space for a record player and the records we were going to acquire. From the other crate we retrieved only the dainty Japanese tea set. Using Gerda's sewing machine, I made curtains for the two windows. We bought a refrigerator from Eric Anderson's. The furniture arrived from Sydney on time. All was in readiness.

Saturday 28 July 1962 was a clear, cool and, unfortunately, windy winter's day. It was also an extremely hectic day. It was the day our bedsitter was ready to be occupied. From early morning till ninety minutes before the wedding ceremony, which luckily was not until five p.m., we were in Holmes Crescent, Campbell, putting everything into place: the furniture, the kitchenware, the bedding, our clothes. We moved in, fully and completely, with everything we owned. All in the one go. On our wedding day.

Then it was back to Max and Gerda's. Chris went to pick up the flowers, but what they were I cannot remember. According to the photos, they could have been orchids. I had washed my hair in the morning and run around all day with it in rollers. Now Gerda's hairdresser friend came to do my hair and fasten the veil. Gerda helped me with the dress. I did not wear make-up. It was frowned upon when and where I grew up; in fact, painting your nails or wearing lipstick were said to be the province of doubtful, if not loose, women. Perfume was allowed, but in moderation. And so, for most of my life I have managed without make-up. I noticed that here in Australia women powdered their faces (and often forgot about the neck) and many wore rather bright lipstick. They also did their own hair, which meant that – like I did on my wedding day – they could often be seen with their hair in rollers, perhaps while gardening, occasionally even at the shops. Women also shaved their legs and under their arms. All of this was new to me.

So here I was in my pale eggshell satin wedding dress with its long slender sleeves and its lacy neckline, looking at myself in the mirror. Gerda had left the room. I was alone. 'This is it,' girl, I said to myself. 'The day has come. There's no way back now.'

My musings were interrupted by a knock on the door. Chris had come to fetch me. I think he liked what he saw. Gerda drove us to the church in their light brown undecorated Holden station wagon. The children were with her parents for the day.

We sat in the back seat holding hands. Gerda said little, nor did we, just occasionally Chris would squeeze my hand. We arrived at the church before any guests had turned up. Were we so eager? Or was it that inbred German sense of punctuality? So Gerda took us for a drive around the suburbs of Reid and Ainslie. Max, one of the two best men, made his own way to the church. The other best man was Ian,

Chris's colleague who had lent us his green VW beetle. There were no bridesmaids. I was virtually alone among strangers.

Pastor Röhrs's wife played the organ as Chris and I slowly walked down the aisle. There was a beautiful flower arrangement, and there must have been a photographer, as some professional-looking photographs grace our album. The ceremony lasted less than half an hour. The vows were in both languages and I had to try very hard to keep my voice steady. The rings then went back on where they had been before; and while we knelt for the blessing my knees would not stop trembling. At the end, the tiny congregation managed to sing to Mrs Röhrs's accompaniment. Then came the paperwork in the church office, and finally we walked back along the aisle to the sounds of the wedding march, out into the setting sun and the winter wind.

Before the group photo was taken on the church steps, I was introduced to those guests I had not met before – the wives or girlfriends of Chris's colleagues. No one extended a hand to me; it was just nods and smiles all around as they said their pleased-to-meet-yous and their congratulations. The only hugs came from Gerda and Roma. Perhaps the others weren't quite sure how to behave towards this strange woman who, in her short wedding dress, had walked down the aisle on her future husband's arm. The group photo shows sixteen guests. No one had thrown confetti or rice – I didn't even know that that was a tradition here. Nor had anyone tied tin cans to the car.

Then it was time to go to the Ainslie Hotel for celebratory champagne. Dinner followed, with the menu very much reflecting the taste of the times. This was it:

Cream of Tomato Soup
Spaghetti Bolognaise
Chicken Maryland or Fillet Steak and Mushrooms or Lobster Newburg
Fruit Salad and Ice Cream or Apple Slice and Cream

The cost? Twenty-five shillings per person.

The wedding cake, which was not a wedding cake in the traditional sense but a German torte with chocolate and cream, especially created for us by Gerda's father, a pastry cook, was served with coffee and tea after the meal. Unfortunately, there was no piece of cake for the guests to take home.

There were two speeches over dinner, the first one by Ian, but what he said I do not remember; perhaps I didn't even understand it all – he was one of the mumblers. The second speech, appropriately, was by my new husband who, on behalf of his wife, thanked the guests and said whatever newly married husbands used to say then on their wedding day.

We had arranged with the hotel management that after our dinner in a private area, we would join the other hotel guests for the Saturday night dinner dance. This happened by the simple removal of a partition. Bruce Lansley and his band, three musicians in total, were a well-known Canberra band at the time. They welcomed us with a special little fanfare and then played the wedding waltz. All the Saturday-night diners looked on as the two of us glided across the dance floor.

In the course of the evening, among the talking, the eating and the drinking, my eyes occasionally strayed down the table and I looked at the faces of these strangers who were guests at my wedding. Where was my family? Where were my friends? This was my wedding day, and I was among strangers. Or was I the stranger? It was a peculiar feeling, unreal once more. Yes, family and friends were far away and I missed them terribly, but it had been my decision to come here and get married. I would do my best to make it work. I would endeavour not to remain a stranger in this town or in this country.

Some congratulatory cards had arrived from overseas, even a telegram. Interflora had delivered two bouquets of flowers, one from each of our families. I have no recollection of the wedding gifts the guests had brought, if indeed they had brought any; perhaps they chipped in towards expenses. Chris does not remember either. Understandably, there were no telephone calls from overseas; not only because costs would have been prohibitively high, but also because we did not own a telephone.

We left the party around ten p.m. and returned to our tiny bedsitter; the first night in our first home in this new country of ours. We put a record on, had a glass of wine and talked about the future.

Chris had taken two weeks' leave for our honeymoon, and once again Ian had lent us his green VW beetle. We had decided to have a quiet and relaxing Sunday after all the excitement of the past weeks and leave on our honeymoon on the Monday. When our landlord and his wife came downstairs on Sunday afternoon to wish us all the best and Mrs S addressed me as Frau Acker, for a moment I did not know to whom she was talking.

With regard to married names, what I did not know then, but discovered shortly after, was that a married woman was usually referred to not just as Mrs Smith, which I thought was the proper way, but as Mrs John Smith. It was as if by marrying, a woman lost not only her maiden name but her given name as well, like losing her whole identity. She almost did not exist, except as a kind of addendum to her husband. At the time, and for quite a few years to come, the social pages in the newspaper were certainly full of Mrs John Smiths and Mrs Robert Balls. Was I going to be Mrs Chris Acker? How strange! In Germany I would have been Frau Margitta Acker.

On Monday morning after breakfast, we packed the car and headed east. Even though it was winter, we wanted to see the sea, walk along a beach, hear the waves, feel the wind in our faces. So along the King's Highway we went, through Bungendore and Braidwood, towns that looked a bit forlorn amongst the never-ending paddocks. There were still some unsealed patches of highway, and what was sealed was certainly narrower and bumpier than it is today. The drive down Clyde Mountain with its many twists and turns was a rather scary but also an exhilarating experience. The forests along the way were something to behold: the tall eucalyptus trees, the coarse bracken, the feathery ferns, the intrepid climbers, creepers and lianas. It looked like a jungle to me. We stopped several times so I could take a closer look. It was all so different from the trees I knew from the other side of the world.

At Nelligen, the road finished at the edge of a wide river. There was no bridge across the Clyde River; a vehicle ferry plied its leisurely path across the water.

Batemans Bay was a disappointment: it had a couple of motels, none of which was anywhere near the ocean. I for one was definitely looking at the town with German eyes: I was looking for a beach promenade, for cafés, a hotel or a motel with water views. There was nothing of the sort. So Batemans Bay was out. We would keep looking for a promenade and a motel by the water's edge. We drove south. We had heard mention of Sunpatch, people had beach houses there. Perhaps that would be the place to go. Sunpatch – Tomakin today – was an even greater disappointment: it consisted of nothing but vacant lots and the odd beach shack. Some of the structures that stood there at the time certainly would not qualify to be called houses today. So we fled north, as our ultimate destination would once again be Sydney. We found no promenade anywhere, nor did we find a hotel or motel with water views. In Nowra we gave up. It was dark by then, and we were tired. We settled for the next-best motel where all that was available was a family room with a double and three single beds. At least it was spacious.

From Nowra we drove up Cambewarra Mountain towards Kangaroo Valley. Again we had to stop on the way: here cabbage tree palms lined the road. I simply had to take a photo of these exotic-looking specimens as well as of the view that spread out before us. The kiosk at the top of the mountain with its fabulous lookout was a very modest affair, but the lookout more than compensated for the kiosk's shortcomings: no decent coffee, no cake, just tea and soft drinks; and meat pies (by now I knew what they were).

In Sydney, this time, we explored the coastline and the beaches rather than the city. We walked along some of its beautiful beaches, watching the waves roll in, and I thought of the Baltic Sea on the shores of which I had spent many a summer's day of my childhood. I made a comparison with what I'd known: this here was wilder, younger, newer, more exciting. The whole continent was like that, I felt, not just the beaches and the ocean.

We stood at Captain Cook's landing place and watched the wild surf thrash onto rocks. It was here that I again realised how little I knew about Australia, its history, its people, its geography and its institutions. I decided to do something about that lack of knowledge as soon as we returned; so the first book I bought when we were back in Canberra was Manning Clark's *A Short History of Australia*.

For a very special treat, Chris took me out to dinner at one of Sydney's few nightclubs, Chequers, where we dined in grand style – or so at least it seemed to one who had never before been to anything vaguely resembling a nightclub. Later in the evening we watched a revue; the troupe was called Les Girls, but despite their beautiful dresses and their intricately made-up faces, these girls were definitely not female. An eye opener!

After Sydney, we headed west to the Blue Mountains where we stayed at a motel in Katoomba, now legally as Mr and Mrs. We explored the area's famous sights, and as it was midweek and midwinter, we mostly had the lookouts and the cliff walks to ourselves. It snowed during the night, and when breakfast was delivered through the hatch the next morning, we caught a glimpse of a white world outside. Beyond Katoomba, somewhere along the way we even found enough snow to have a snowball fight; but overall the white wonder did not last the day.

For our return trip to Canberra we chose the back road via the Jenolan Caves and Taralga to Goulburn, most of which was gravel, not much more than a farm track, really. For all of its one hundred and fifty kilometres or so, we encountered fewer than a handful of vehicles and only occasionally did we spot a farm. Very lonely country indeed for someone who had come from crowded Europe. Whenever we came to a creek crossing where water ran across the road – and there were several – I was fearful that we might get stuck. I would get out of the car and probe the depth of the creek with a stick before Chris could drive through; after all, we were only driving a VW beetle and someone else's at that. Despite my timidity, I found this part of the trip exciting and adventurous.

When we returned to Canberra after a week's travel, we had done 777 miles and it seemed to me as if we had been on a grand journey through the continent. When I checked the map, we had only seen a minuscule part of it. So much more was waiting!

The wedding was over. The honeymoon was over, another week at home and Chris had to return to work. Then I would be alone in the bedsitter, at least from Monday to Friday.

# 3

## Settling in – guineas and swear words

For the next two years and nine months, the single-garage-size flat was our home. It may have been tiny, but it was a cosy place: the kitchen shelves held a set of bright canisters and a set of gleaming new saucepans; a small collection of prickly cacti graced the window sill; and colourful sunsets could often be seen from the window. On the other side of the wardrobe/divider, our combined living and sleeping area had two comfortable easy chairs, a coffee table and a sofa bed. There were a few books, and there was our precious radio. Things were going well.

Canberra's population at the end of 1962 was less than 70,000, spread over the various suburbs of what are now North and South Canberra. The place was a hive of activity; construction work was going on in many places: new roads and bridges, a dam, shops and office buildings and, most of all, houses were going up everywhere, centrally as well as on the town's fringes. There were two hostels on Capital Hill, the Hillside and the Capital Hill Hostel, housing an international medley of men needed by the construction industry. There were other hostels too, more upmarket ones for public servants: for single men and single women and possibly even families.

Max and Gerda were eager to show us around, to give us a taste of what this young town was like and would be like in the future. One Sunday afternoon Max parked the car on a dirt track, where a cycle path now runs below the Tuggeranong Parkway. From there we had a good view over the construction site of the Scrivener Dam wall, not far from the historic mansion where the governor general, the representative of the Queen, lived. It seemed rather strange to me that her influence reached as far as the other side of the globe. But then again, Australia had once been a British colony and to many Australians Britain was still 'home'; it was their mother country, I was told.

Max then took us – four adults and two small children, no seat belts yet and certainly no child restraints – around the central area of Canberra to give us an idea of the extent of the future lake. It was hard to imagine such a large body of water where at that time there was only a thin rivulet with the important-sounding name of Molonglo River; where there were piles of dirt, piles of rocks, snaking vehicle tracks and patches of pale grass. After the dam was finished in 1963 and the valves were closed, the people of Canberra were eagerly waiting for the lake to fill. But it seemed to take forever, because rainfall was too scarce over the summer to make any noticeable impression apart from a few larger puddles. When the rains finally came, in the autumn of 1964, they came hard and heavy, and in a matter of days Canberra suddenly had this expansive, promising and refreshing body of water right in its middle.

In 1962, the only connections between North and South Canberra were a low-level crossing over the Molonglo at Acton and a bumpy wooden bridge that crossed the river a short distance upstream. The tall concrete Commonwealth Avenue Bridge opened in 1963 over a dusty lake bed and the Kings Avenue one a year or so later. There were no traffic lights anywhere; they did not turn up until a few years later, the first ones being installed along Northbourne Avenue. The general traffic rule was that one always gave way to the right.

I liked the way Canberra was spread out; it felt more like an accumulation of villages than a city; it certainly had nothing in common with traditional European cities. No person called the city centre home; the city centre housed only shops and offices. Everyone lived in the suburbs.

Although it was winter when we first came to Canberra and many trees and shrubs were bare, the suburbs – particularly the older ones – had a very pleasing look about them. Most lawns, although a bit dull, were neatly trimmed, most garden beds tidy and well planted. Occasionally, though, it was obvious that gardening was not one of the homeowner's priorities or interests. Individual blocks were spacious, and there were no front fences, giving every street a parklike appearance. There were no footpaths in the suburbs either. Hardly anyone walked anywhere anyway. Did everyone own a car? I wondered. When in spring the flowers burst forth and the deciduous trees put on their green finery, the whole of Canberra, or at least the old suburbs, looked like one big park with houses sprinkled in between, and letter boxes standing to attention at the edges of nature strips.

One spring day, walking through the reserve behind our street, I chanced upon Mt Pleasant, near the Royal Military College at Duntroon. What a view! The whole town was at my feet. To the left were green fields dissected by the Molonglo River, with the airport in the distance; to the right was the city centre bordered by the hulk of Black Mountain (then without the Telstra tower); and on the far horizon was the chain of mountains that had fascinated me right from the beginning. I felt a great affinity with the landscape. It felt right to be here.

During our first year in Canberra we became friends with another German couple, Konrad and Hildegard, who had been married only a year; their baby girl was born on our wedding day. Konrad, a cabinetmaker, had built our first piece of furniture: the cabinet for our imported wireless and our future record collection. In the true German fashion we visited them at their cottage in Fyshwick – Konrad had a workshop there and had been permitted to build a cottage for his small family next to it – for Sunday afternoon coffee and cake. We were all dressed in our Sunday best. Sometimes these coffee and cake sessions extended into the evening when Hildegard served up cold meats and cheese and bread. This was the German way: a hot meal in the middle of the day and sandwiches in the evening; quite unlike the Australian way.

We rarely invited anyone to our little bedsitter; there just wasn't space for more than two guests. It was easier to take a cake or some snacks along when we dropped in on our German friends. We invited Ian and Roma once and were invited to their home at Canberra Boys' Grammar School for dinner. When we arrived, I exchanged smiles and nods with Ian, but Roma greeted me in what I thought was the French way of greeting: cheek to cheek, both sides, and blowing a kiss into the air. But Roma's way was very rare at the time, and I did not come across it again for many years. Now, of course, it's all the rage; and not only between women, but just as normal between men and women, and even between men.

Every Friday night Chris came home in the company car which we were allowed to use over the weekend. So sometimes we went for Sunday drives into the countryside around Canberra, just the two of us, exploring some of the many back roads leading in all directions to areas such as the Queanbeyan River, Captains Flat, Wee Jasper or even Cooma. There was so much to explore.

Having the use of a vehicle allowed us another type of weekend entertainment: an evening at the Starlight Drive-In at Watson. We could have gone to the cinema in Manuka or Civic, but the drive-in was a novelty. We even went in the winter months, when – along with the speaker – patrons were provided with a heater to hang inside the car. It was always quite cosy. The other reason we preferred the drive-in over the cinema was that in the cinema, before the show began, the national anthem was played and patrons rose and stood until the strains of 'God Save the Queen' had faded away. What did the Queen have to do with us and a visit to the movies? It seemed strange.

On cold or rainy Sundays, when there was little else to do, we stayed home, listened to the radio or played records or read. Apart from Manning Clark's *A Short History of Australia*, I was eager to read more about Australia and by Australian writers. That's how I initially got to know Patrick White's books and those by George Johnston and Frank Hardy, and many others as the years went by. It was on occasions like these that the Japanese tea set was brought out, and we had afternoon tea in style. Many years later, when the novelty had worn off and practicalities had taken over, I took the tea set to an antique dealer at the Yarralumla brickworks. He paid me $25 for it. Today, cups and saucers seem to have all but disappeared; mugs are the order of the day. Fifty years ago, campers and shearers would have used mugs; the rest of the population had their tea or coffee served in a more sophisticated style.

Gradually, I was getting used to the Australian way of speaking. Not everybody spoke through clenched teeth, after all. But there were some peculiarities. For example, a woman I had met finished many of her sentences with the word 'but', as in 'He went home, but' or 'I never met her, but.' I never found out why this 'but' was where it was and she couldn't explain it, even wondered why I was querying it at all. Maybe it was just the way some people spoke at the time, in the same way as some young people today use the word 'like' in all sorts of places, appropriate and inappropriate.

And then there were swear words. There seemed to be some strange aura about them. And a lot of hypocrisy! Chris had a colleague who maintained that if he ever heard his kids use a swear word – I believe 'bloody' and 'damn' were considered the height of awfulness – he would wash their mouths out with soap. Yet, according to Chris, he himself used those words quite liberally. Apparently it was okay for a man, a 'bloke', to swear, as long as it was not in front of the kids or the ladies. There are, of course, similar bad words in the German language, but they don't seem to have that same status of expressing badness or boldness or whatever as they do in the English language. Our parents never used them, nor did we or anyone else we knew. On the other hand, I noticed that Australians used 'please' and 'thank you' a great deal; more, anyway, than we were used to. And 'sorry' as well. They were a polite people, these Australians, I thought.

As already mentioned, shopping opportunities in Canberra in the early 1960s were very limited: apart from Civic, there was Kingston and there was Manuka, and they seemed a long way away from

Campbell. Our first pieces of furniture had come from Sydney. My wedding dress had come from there. So had Chris's suit. We had J.B. Youngs in Garema Place and a few other shops in that part of Civic. But then, one day, there was the Monaro Mall. What an exciting event it was when the mall opened: here was David Jones stretched over three floors with a café near the entrance; here were dress shops and shoe shops and jewellers; here were escalators and lifts; all those things that are now part of our normal shopping experience but were then very much a novelty. We rode up and down the escalator just for the fun of it.

And what about food shops? The Germans are fussy about their bread, their sausages, their cuts of meat. Food shops were geared very much to the English, or perhaps the Australian, palate: the only bread was the doughy white stuff, the sausages were of the greasy pork kind or that tasteless, flavourless devon for sandwiches, and no butcher seemed to know how to cut beef so the German housewife could cook proper *Rouladen*. The Blue Moon Café and Delicatessen in Civic carried some continental smallgoods, and that is where we – and many other migrants – went for salamis and liverwurst or tinned imported foods, and even some good coffee.

For the meat and a more appealing range of smallgoods, Gerda introduced us to Vicky's in Queanbeyan. Vicky – or whatever his real name was – was a Polish migrant who had a pretty good idea how to cut the meat – pork, beef or veal – for his German customers. Lamb, on the other hand, was something the Germans preferred to avoid. Many a German man had first come across lamb in the form of tough and greasy mutton at the Bonegilla migrant hostel or a construction hostel in the Snowy Mountains. Our landlady shunned it for precisely that reason: her husband would never eat it, she said, and she had no idea how to prepare it. Chris liked lamb and one Sunday prepared a roast leg of lamb with a very tasty gravy. He gave our landlady a couple of slices of meat and a couple of ladles of gravy without telling her what type of meat it was. They ate it and liked it and couldn't believe that they had just eaten lamb. Whether they ever had it again, we do not know.

Shopping required familiarity with the currency. And what a peculiar currency they had here. I had been to England on two occasions, so was familiar with pounds, shillings and pence – and even guineas. How cumbersome it was to add up your income and expenses, to multiply and divide without the simple swiftness of the decimal system! Twelve pence to a shilling, twenty shillings to a pound, and twenty-one shillings to a guinea. Luckily, the decimal currency system was in the pipeline and was introduced in 1966, when ten shillings became a dollar. What a relief! And yet there were many Australians who hankered after the old system and for a while kept converting the cost of things from the new to the old currency.

Something similar happened – and in some instances it lasted a very long time – when the metric system was introduced a few years later for all weights and measures. Forever after, it seemed, people kept talking in inches, feet and miles; some of them still do so today. For us, kilometres, metres, centimetres, millimetres – it was all so familiar, and so easy.

And then there was the queue: at banks, in shops, wherever people were waiting to be attended to, a queue formed, and everyone in that queue waited patiently. This was also a peculiarly British habit; us Germans just tended to push and shove a bit or pretend we hadn't seen the others waiting. Now, of course, in banks, airports and even cinemas, queues are properly organised via posts and ribbons.

Our landlord had allowed us some space in the back garden for a vegetable patch. It wasn't very big but during the summer months it provided us with some of the vegetables we knew from home, but which were not readily available here, although the seeds were, like leek and kohlrabi. But we also grew a few carrots, beans, lettuce and radishes.

Then we acquired a pet. At Konrad's workshop in Fyshwick, a young magpie had fallen out of its nest and injured one of its wings.

Konrad constructed a sizeable cage and we took the young bird back to our landlord's back garden. The bird became very attached to us. When we were home, we often kept it in the kitchen, where it hopped around on the floor and eventually went to sleep on its piece of carpet in the corner. If someone came, it would shriek and try to attack the visitor's feet. But most of the time the magpie was in its cage in the back garden, safe from other magpies. When we occasionally let it hop around in the back garden, it was always wary of other magpies whose territory it knew it was invading. It loved playing around the garden hose and the sprinkler, but one day, after it had pulled out every single seedling that our landlady had planted in her vegetable garden – and she was not amused – it was clear to us that we could no longer keep the bird. We were rather sad when we took it out to the CSIRO station on the Barton Highway.

For reasons unknown to me now, right from the beginning I was very keen to obtain my driver's licence, even though we did not yet own a car. Why that was in any way important at the time, I do not recall. As I already had a German driver's licence, someone suggested that I might obtain an Australian one without undergoing any tests. But no such luck. I had to do both the theoretical and the practical test, and I failed. I failed the practical test because of some silly parking oversight. Naturally, I was disappointed, but determined to try again. Less than a year later, after we had our own car, I again fronted up at the traffic office with both my German driver's licence and my marriage certificate. Whether the rules had changed in the meantime, or just the staff at the counter, I will never know, but I received my longed-for driving authority there and then. No more tests.

Apart from the basic necessities, one of our early acquisitions was a sewing machine. I was keen to make my own clothes, as ready-made clothes were not only expensive, there wasn't a great range to choose from. The first dress I made was a little black dress, the sort of dress a woman simply had to have – as far as I knew anyway – if she were to go to the theatre or a cocktail party. I never wore it to a cocktail party because of lack of opportunity, but I wore it to the theatre, or rather – on a first occasion – to the opera.

The Sydney Opera Company, I think that is what it was then called, was coming to Canberra in the winter of 1963 to present *La Traviata*. The venue was the Albert Hall. Chris donned the suit he had worn for our wedding. I wore my little black dress, high heels, of course, and my winter coat. We knew the Albert Hall was not big; we had so far only seen it from the outside. So we expected something akin to a small opera house with tiered seating, a small raised stage, a smaller-than-usual orchestra, but an orchestra nonetheless. We also expected a cloakroom. That was our first disappointment. There was no cloakroom; patrons just walked through the foyer into the hall with their coats on, taking them off inside, holding them on their laps or putting them on the floor. Of course, there was no proper stage, no tiered seating, no small orchestra. There were just rows and rows of hard chairs in front of which stood a grand piano, and behind the piano there was in fact something that vaguely resembled a stage: a sort of raised platform. Our hearts sank. This was supposed to be an opera presentation? We had forgotten that we were in pioneer country, frontier country as far as the arts were concerned. We must forget our European ways of dreaming up expectations, of looking at things with European eyes, of comparing. This truly was another world.

As the piano hammered away to Verdi's tunes and the singers, among them Robert Gard, sang the familiar tunes, I was reminded of the words an Englishwoman had said to me in London in 1961 when I had told her I would be going to Australia the following year. 'Australia,' she had said, 'why Australia? They have no culture down there, you know.' But I wasn't going to Australia for the culture, I was going there for the adventure.

After the little black dress, my next project was a light grey linen suit trimmed with a darker grey in true Chanel style. This I wore – with matching pale grey handbag and shoes – on some of our Sunday afternoon outings when we went for a stroll in Civic, window shopping or along what was supposed to become the lake, or to visit friends for coffee and cake. In one of our albums there is a photo of me in my Sunday best walking along some dusty track on the bottom of the future Lake Burley Griffin. And after the Chanel suit, I cut up my wedding dress to create a short-sleeved evening dress, just in case an occasion arose at which I could wear it. It did, but not until several years later.

Over the years, I made other suits. I made dresses and blouses, even a new winter coat. I also knitted jumpers and cardigans, and crocheted a poncho, until eventually it became cheaper to buy a ready-made dress or a knitted jumper than to buy the material and sit down and make it.

What I found rather amusing on the clothing front were the men in their shorts and their knee-high white or beige socks. Taxi drivers wore them, and bank clerks and technicians. In fact, it was like a uniform: the distance between the top rim of the socks and the bottom rim of the shorts was set to be a certain number of inches so as not to show too much leg. And men never wore short socks with their shorts; that was a definite faux pas.

A month after my wedding and not much more than two months after my arrival in Australia, I had a full-time job, so my days of leisure were over. While the five weeks before the wedding had been hectic, once we had returned from our honeymoon and Chris had returned to work, I had time on my hands. These weeks in limbo were a strangely quiet time, a time of waiting. Waiting for Chris to come home on Fridays; waiting to find a job; waiting for letters from overseas; waiting for the bus to take me away from our isolated basement dwelling to the city centre for some 'life', or as far as Lyneham to visit Gerda.

Much of that waiting time I filled with writing letters. Initially they were thank-you letters to family and friends in which I told them about the wedding and about my new life in this far away land. Usually the letters were many pages long and my hands were often aching with cramps from holding the pen. There was just so much to tell. Only rarely did I use an aerogram – the cheapest way to send a letter overseas

– and if I did, its one and a half pages were crammed to the margins. Letters from overseas were, of course, always eagerly awaited; if they contained a photo or two, the excitement was even greater.

I missed having a girlfriend; someone with whom to share those things that only women can share with each other; someone with similar experiences to mine – newly married, new to the country, keen to have a go. Gerda was helpful but, in this instance, did not quite fit the bill: she had a family to look after, a house and garden to maintain, and Lyneham was a fair distance from Campbell. I certainly had my homesick moments, but I tried not to dwell on them.

Once I was working, however, the weekdays seemed to fly. And so did the weekends when Chris was home. Later, when the telecommunications project had finished in May 1963 and Chris had found work in Canberra, our life took on a more normal pattern.

I was endeavouring to be a good housewife. I understood that to be an important role in my life: a good housewife and, perhaps later, a good mother. That I could possibly have something called a 'career' was never a consideration. I was happy to go to work, to have a job, so as to contribute to family finances.

After our shopping sprees on Friday nights – often followed by socialising – Saturday was housekeeping day. That's when I – properly attired in an apron – cleaned the bedsitter from top to bottom: every shelf was wiped and every skirting board. We didn't own a vacuum cleaner and I sometimes borrowed the landlady's. At other times it was a broom and dustpan job. While I was busy indoors, Chris attended to the garden patch, polished our shoes or cleaned out the car. If the car needed to be washed, we drove out to Point Hut crossing on the Murrumbidgee River, parked the vehicle in the water that ran over the low level crossing and washed it there and then (without detergent!). The low-level crossing really was low-level then; some years later a concrete causeway was built over the old low-level crossing, but if the river was in flood, the road would still be closed due to high volumes of water.

Being a good housewife, and a good German housewife at that, meant being good at cooking. This really was not my forte. At home, the kitchen and the meals had been entirely my mother's domain, and as a student, cooking in my room on a single hotplate, I only managed to produce very basic and totally uninteresting meals. Here now was my challenge! During the first year, when Chris was away during the week, I continued to prepare basic meals, at the same time leafing through my one and only recipe book to find more interesting meals for the weekend. For more variety, I invested in an Australian cookery book. Lucky for me, Chris had an interest in cooking, and on weekends we often prepared our meals together, or he showed me how to do certain things.

It was not always easy using a German cookbook and Australian ingredients or vice versa. Things didn't necessarily gel: measurements were different – ounces and pounds, perhaps cups, instead of grams. Sometimes ingredients were simply not available here. For example, German cake recipes specified a packet of baking powder or a packet of vanilla sugar. How much was in a packet? You could not buy such a thing as a packet of vanilla sugar. And when it came to measuring a cup of butter, I thought that a rather stupid idea, because first you squash the butter into the measuring cup, then you scrape it out again. Weighing it on a set of scales would have been so much simpler, either in grams or even in ounces.

Being a good housewife, for me, also entailed keeping track of expenses. When Chris came home with his weekly pay, the money would be divided up: so much would go for rent (once we had used up the advance for finishing the flat), and so much for housekeeping – that is, food and related expenses. We both allowed ourselves some pocket money; the rest would go in the bank. Meticulously I kept a record of all household expenses and never rested (or rarely, anyway) until it all balanced out at the end of the week. Fortunately for my sanity, I did not keep up that habit for very long.

Any payments that were due, for example for a car loan, were made by cheque. For such a loan, we had a booklet with as many slips as there were repayments to be made. Each slip had all relevant details printed on it; so by the due date, one simply mailed off the slip with the cheque or handed it in to the bank. Most other payments, say for the purchase of a sewing machine, could also be made by cheque, although cash was preferred. Credit cards had not been invented then. As far as our savings in the bank were concerned, we had a Bank of New South Wales (now Westpac) savings book, where debits and credits were recorded. And this savings book could be used at any Bank of NSW branch in the country – signature matching was sufficient ID.

Through Max and Gerda we had learned of the German Reading Room located upstairs in the Bailey Arcade, which later became the foundation for the Goethe Institut. They also introduced us to the German Club, established in 1961, whose clubhouse was under construction at the edge of town, at Narrabundah. Until the building was finished, club functions, get-togethers and meetings were held in various church and community halls. Somewhere out near Lake George, there was a place called Karl's Inn, where Saturday-night dinner dances were held, the clientele being almost exclusively German, or at least German-speaking. There you could eat German food and listen or dance to German music. We occasionally went there with Max and Gerda and some of their friends. Once or twice a group of us drove to the coast to spend a weekend at a restaurant cum guest house at Jamberoo, near Kiama, which was run by a German couple and had a very authentic German feel to it. The ties to home were still strong.

Generally, the restaurant scene all those decades ago was, with very few exceptions, very monotonous. There were pubs and clubs; there was the occasional speciality restaurant, mostly Chinese; but it was all rather basic and unexciting compared to the immense variety that is available today.

Our circle of friends slowly extended beyond the German-speaking crowd. With colleagues from Chris's work we sometimes went to the Queanbeyan Leagues Club for an evening's entertainment. The club was a very popular venue for Canberra residents not only for the oh-so-fashionable dinner dances but to play the poker machines, which were then not allowed in the ACT. Gambling was considered a vice that the Canberra population had to be protected from, because many a soul inclined to gambling might spend their evenings, perhaps even their days and sometimes their fortunes, at a club's poker machines. We liked the club mostly for its inexpensive meals and its dinner dances. There would be six or eight of us at a table, the men drinking their beer, the women sipping a shandy or perhaps a Barossa Pearl or a Liebfrauwein or some other sweet and often sparkling wine. Wine wasn't really in then. Women may have preferred it over their Pimms No. 1, but a real man stuck to his beer. Plonk was what wine was often called, especially the fortified variety which was most often sold by the flagon (two litres).

Between the various courses, we danced, but only with our own partners. In Germany it would have been appropriate, and polite, for the men at the table to dance at least once with every female in the party. On one occasion, when Chris and I were on the dance floor, the band leader called out that the next dance would be the Pride of Erin. We had no idea what that was and continued to waltz across the floor until we were tapped on the shoulder by a fellow dancer who told us to either get in line and do what one was supposed to do in the Pride of Erin or get off the dance floor. We chose the latter, then watched the goings-on, so that in future we would know how to behave.

At my first job I became friends with an Englishman, a technician by the name of Shad. Every Friday night, Shad and his wife Pat held open house at their home in Dickson. Shad and Pat had four children, yet the friends who turned up on Friday nights were either single or newly married, people Shad had met along the way and, perhaps, considered lonely and in need of friends. During the war, Shad had been a bomber pilot; he had flown over and dropped bombs on German cities. Our countries had been enemies not so long ago, but now we were in Australia; this was another world, another time. It was always a happy crowd at their Dickson home; sometimes we were only four or five, at other times easily twice that number. There would be much talk, or we listened to music or even danced. And, of course, there was always food and drink, but to my memory no one ever drank too much or stayed too late. After all, Shad and Pat had a young family to look after, not just us young folks.

We would usually go to Shad and Pat's after the shops had closed at nine p.m. In the early years, Friday-night shopping hours were very strange indeed: all shops closed at five-thirty p.m. and opened again an hour later. This was so that sales staff could have their dinner, or 'tea' as it was then called. Where did shoppers spend the time between the closing and reopening of the shop doors? We lived close to Civic and went home after work, had a bite to eat and then went out again. But it wasn't that easy for everyone.

Perhaps some frequented the pubs. But they had odd hours, too. They closed at six p.m., or at least stopped serving drinks at that time. What a strange arrangement! Stranger still did I find the fact that women were only allowed in a certain area of the pub called the ladies' lounge, a rather unfriendly, heavily curtained and carpeted room desperately in need of fresh air. Men were at least conditionally allowed in the ladies' domain, yet the opposite was totally unthinkable. Some women, particularly the older generation, accompanied their husbands to the pub but remained outside in the car, often passing the time knitting or crocheting. The husband came out once in a while and supplied the wife with a drink, non-alcoholic most likely. I assume the positive side of this arrangement was that he was sure she remained sober while he could drink to his heart's content, because he had someone to take him safely home. Or, as these were still pre-breathalyser test times, he may have insisted on driving himself rather than be seen with his wife at the wheel; or rather 'the missus' or 'the wife'. Did Australian men ever say 'my wife'?

There seemed to be some kind of segregation of the sexes in this country, I sometimes felt. Were men afraid of women? Did they feel uncomfortable in their presence? Or simply more at home in the company of other blokes? At parties this was particularly noticeable: men and women often occupied separate areas: the men in the garden or on the veranda, the women in the lounge or, even more likely, in the kitchen. At Shad and Pat's, however, things seemed to be more relaxed between us young people.

When Shad and Pat were having family problems, the Friday-night group gradually dissolved. By then the Monaro Mall had become a permanent fixture on the shopping circuit, and we often met some of our German friends at the café at David Jones, where we drank coffee, talked and smoked until closing time. Sometimes the evening's socialising continued at one or the other's home. Among these friends were Hans and Ilse, who were also friends of Max and Gerda's. In fact, Max and Hans and Chris had come to Australia on the same migrant ship way back in 1955. Everyone in this crowd smoked but me; and as I did not want to be the odd one out, I puffed away as well. I never really enjoyed it. Luckily, smoking eventually became a dirty word, a dirty habit; I had given it away long before then, but it took Chris to the early 1980s before he gave up.

I have been in Australia, in Canberra, for fifty years now. It has taken me about half that time to get used to having Christmas in the summer. Our first Christmas was a disaster. We had lots of little presents for each other; a parcel had come from overseas; we had sent Christmas cards and gifts to the families overseas; we had even purchased a Christmas tree and decorated it. What strange shapes those radiata pines had! It was very difficult to fasten candles to its branches, and by candles, I mean real ones, not little electric lights. Following the German tradition, we celebrated on Christmas Eve. We played our one and only record of Christmas carols, and I cried my eyes out. The next day we drove to the coast. It was unbearably hot, and a glaring sun, burning sand and a pounding surf certainly did not give me a Christmassy feeling. On the contrary; there were more tears.

A German Christmas begins with the four Advent Sundays: there is the advent wreath with its four candles. Late in the afternoon of the first Advent Sunday, when it is already dark outside, one candle is lit on the wreath and left to flicker for a time while the family has their afternoon coffee. The following Sunday two candles are lit, a week later three, and finally all four on the Sunday before Christmas. The Christmas tree with its twelve candles – one for each month of the year – is then lit for the first time on Christmas Eve. Then there is St Nicholas Day on 6 December, when the children hang a stocking or sock outside their bedroom door and find it filled with goodies the next morning, usually some sweets or an orange, at least that's what it was during my childhood; today there's probably much more.

In the German winter, when the days are short and it is cold outside, everyone prefers to be indoors, near the warming hearth and the flickering candles. It is an atmosphere conducive to reflection, to stillness. Whereas here it is summer, a time of partying, of fun and frolicking, of silly hats and noisy crackers. The carol 'Silent Night', to me, encompasses the Christmas atmosphere in Germany; in contrast, 'Jingle Bells' is much more indicative of the Australian Christmas spirit.

After that first tearful Christmas, we decided to do things differently. For the next few years, on Christmas Eve we went out for dinner to the Carousel on Red Hill, one of Canberra's very few quality restaurants. It was a magic place. Not only were the food and the service excellent, the views were simply superb. On several occasions a thunderstorm was brewing over Canberra, there was lightning all around and roaring thunder: an awe-inspiring and memorable spectacle.

*Our wedding, July 1962.*

*Washing the car at Point Hut Crossing, summer 1962/63.*

*On the way to Adelaide, late December 1962.*

*Breakfast at Old Jindabyne, early January 1963.*

*Wily gums, summer 1962/63.*

*Bush picnic, summer 1962/63.*

*Pet magpie, summer 1962/63.*

*Gate on the Rules Point Road, Easter 1963.*

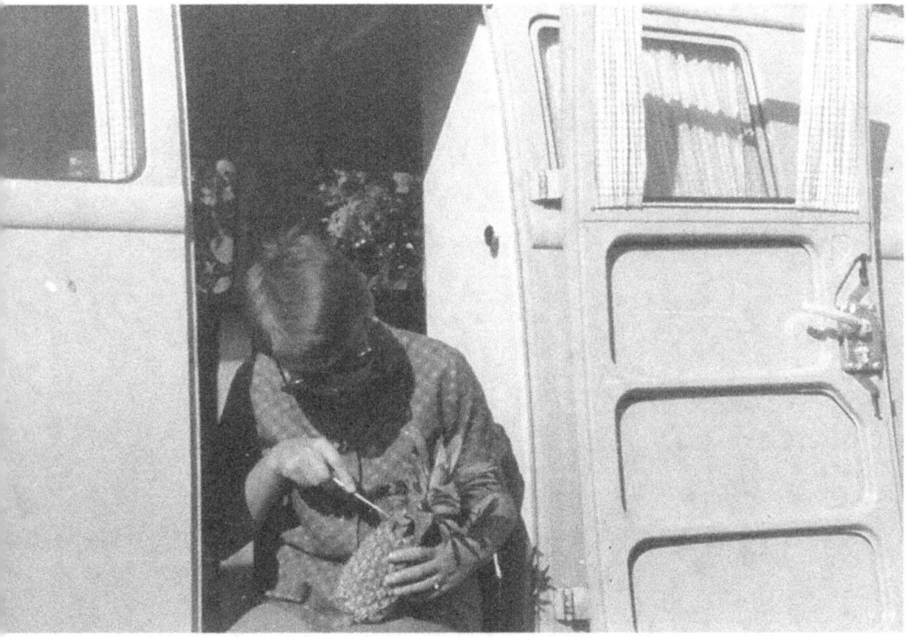

*My first pineapple, May 1963.*

*Cacti on the windowsill, winter 1963.*

*A Sunday stroll across the site of the future Lake Burley Griffin, winter 1963.*

*Our radio and my little black dress, winter 1963.*

*Our house, winter 1965.*

*Concreting in our backyard, spring 1965.*

*Sanding our lounge room, summer 1965/66.*

*Weeding the lawn, summer 1965/66.*

# 4

# Fishing and other adventures in the bush

Right from the beginning, I was keen to explore our new surroundings. At first it was Max and Gerda who showed us around the growing capital; then, with Chris's work car, a Holden panel van, available to us every weekend, we ventured into the area surrounding Canberra, and once we had our own car, we explored places at the coast – anywhere from Jervis Bay to Eden – and in the Snowy Mountains, as well as eventually heading further north and further south.

Max and Gerda also introduced us to the bush. This word alone was a new concept for me. Bush – to me it was a shrub, to them it was anything away from the city. Together we went to the Cotter, to Paddys River and to Casuarina Sands on the Murrumbidgee River. There the weir, which was still standing then but was demolished some years later, provided a perfect swimming spot for adults and children alike. We often had picnics out there – another new experience for me, usually a very pleasant one except for the flies. My European eyes may have looked for a café, but of course there was none; just the occasional wooden picnic table and some blackened fireplaces.

Every now and again when we were out in the bush or driving past the sign indicating that Mt Franklin was only some fifty kilometres away, I wished we would turn on to that particular road to go up into the mountains which, I had learned, were called the Brindabellas, a name that rolled off the tongue even more melodiously than Murrumbidgee. The Mt Franklin Road was too rough, I was told when I inquired; it would be too long a drive for a Sunday afternoon. It wasn't until a year or so later, after Max acquired a rattly Land Rover, that we went with him into those mountains, not only to Mt Franklin and its shelter hut, but further afield too: down a narrow, winding and at times heart-stopping track into the lush, remote Brindabella Valley where the clear waters of the Goodradigbee River flowed. This name flowed a bit harder off the tongue than Brindabella or Murrumbidgee.

Chris and I had our very first taste of camping in the bush, of roughing it, when we travelled to Adelaide over the 1962 Christmas break (after the tearful Christmas Day on the beach) in the company car. The telecommunications project was scheduled to finish in a few months and all project staff had been offered positions in either Sydney or Adelaide. Chris's offer was for Adelaide, so we wanted to have a look at the place before making a decision.

It was a long and lonely drive over the Hay Plains, so vast, so empty, always more sky than earth. In northern Germany, where I grew up, the countryside is also very flat, but somehow the sky never appeared so vast – and definitely never so blue. When we reached the fabled Barossa Valley, we missed it altogether, because we were looking for a wine-growing area resembling the sometimes steep, sometimes gently sloping valleys of the Rhine and Moselle rivers. This Barossa Valley was not much of a valley, just gently rolling countryside with a few vineyards. How disappointing!

We arrived in Adelaide on a grey, dull and cool late December day. It could have been just the weather or perhaps the sight of the factory where Chris was supposed to work, but Adelaide did not impress us in the least. No, we didn't want to move there after we had only just put our feet down in Canberra. Of that we were certain. And Chris did not want to work in a factory, no matter what the position. So we turned round.

As we had time, we returned to Canberra by a different and longer route. In the back of the panel van we carried a mattress, some cooking gear, a picnic hamper and an esky. The vehicle's rear door served as our table and the esky as our seat. The esky still exists – and still gets used occasionally. Thus we travelled all the way along the Murray Valley, pulling off the highway somewhere for the night; again passing the already familiar Hume Weir and eventually heading into the mountains. After a long uphill zigzag on a gravel road, we finally came to Dead Horse Gap near Thredbo. We stood next to the sign that indicated Mt Kosciuszko somewhere in the clouds and continued on along the valley past Thredbo with its one chairlift to Jindabyne. Here the dam was under construction, but there was no lake yet. We camped on the village green by the edge of the Snowy River in the old Jindabyne. The people were still going about their daily business, even though they knew that their village was doomed to disappear under the waters of the lake in a few years and a new Jindabyne would rise on the lake's southern shores.

This trip was my first experience of roughing it, and I liked it. Many more were to follow.

In the autumn of 1963 we acquired our first car. We needed a vehicle of our own, and we knew what we wanted. Of course, it had to be a German brand, a Volkswagen, but not a small beetle like we had used on our honeymoon; we wanted a VW kombi van that we were going to fit out for camping. As we did not have the necessary cash to buy the vehicle outright, we had to get a loan from the bank, which was anything but easy. It required a lot of paperwork and several guarantees before we could drive that pale green brand-new vehicle away from the dealer's.

Chris spent several weekends at Konrad's workshop in Fyshwick and, with his help, fitted out the vehicle with cupboards, a table and benches that converted to a bed at night. We had suitable mattresses made, bought sleeping bags, a gas cooker and light and other camping paraphernalia. Now we were ready to explore further afield than Captains Flat or Cooma. Our first trial outing was a Saturday night at Uriarra Crossing. We cooked our evening meal out there, spent a peaceful night in the van and woke to the chorus of birds and the gentle flow of water.

At Easter we headed for Tumut, Talbingo and the Yarrangobilly Caves. There used to be a hotel at the caves then and a campground where we parked our van. The place was almost deserted. But we were surprised at how cold the night was. In the morning, when we sat inside the van drinking our coffee, the water dripped off the ceiling into our cups. But what a beautiful place it was! The poplars were in their finest autumn gold, the sun was out, a gentle breeze whispered in the eucalypts and even the birds were respectfully quiet after their morning wake-up songs. To be virtually alone in such a striking place can be a humbling experience.

Whether any of the caves were accessible then, I do not recall, but we certainly checked out the thermal pool, which at that time was just a big hole in the ground with timbered sides and a sandy bottom. No change rooms or toilets, no wading pool for the kids, just this big hole full of warm water. Over the years we have gone back to Yarrangobilly many times. For a number of years the area was closed to the public. During that time the hotel was shut down and turned into an information centre, and the campground was closed altogether due to environmental concerns. There is now a large picnic area, and the thermal pool has had a massive facelift, including change rooms and toilets, a wading pool and a little waterfall. And there are a number of walking tracks. The area still has its very particular charm.

On that Easter trip we returned from Yarrangobilly Caves via the Rules Point Road, which used to connect the Snowy Mountains Highway with the Brindabella Valley and roughly followed a high-voltage power line of the Snowy Mountains Hydro-Electric Scheme. The gravel track ran partly through private property, and there were a total of twenty-two farm gates to be opened and closed. Quite a task! Once you reached the Brindabella Valley, the narrow winding track across the mountains back to Canberra still had to be tackled. Today one can no longer travel along the full length of the Rules Point Road, because there is now a locked gate at a section of private road near the Brindabella end. Pity! There is a diversion, I believe, but it is said to be a very rough track and it is longer too. And apparently most gates have disappeared and been replaced by grids.

When the telecommunications project eventually finished at the end of May 1963, we took our first real holiday and went north. We wanted to go to Queensland, to the Gold Coast, to Surfers Paradise, where apparently it is always summer. Travelling in our van, stopping at camping grounds or sometimes just away from the road in the bush, was great fun. I felt as if I was on a real adventure, on a journey of exploration. I was seeing a little bit more of the big wide world, and a bigger bit of Australia.

Surfers Paradise in 1963 was not much more than a village along a beautiful wide beach. There was barely a building taller than three or four storeys. Its most upmarket hotel was the Chevron along the main road, and we stopped at a caravan park near there.

One of the best known of the few tourist attractions on the Gold Coast then was the aquarium at Coolangatta, where dolphins and seals were performing. Of course we had to go there. I even volunteered to hold up a fish and wait for the dolphin to fly up out of the water and fetch it. How exciting it all was!

It was there at Surfers Paradise in 1963 that I touched and tasted my very first pineapple. I thought it had a very exotic taste. Later, in the Gold Coast hinterland, we came across a banana plantation. Underneath a little shelter, bananas were waiting for a buyer, but there was no seller in sight: it all worked on an honesty system. Another novelty for me.

In November 1964, while we were still living in our tiny bedsitter, we took another holiday. This time we went south along the coast through Lakes Entrance all the way to Wilsons Promontory and Phillip Island and along the Mornington Peninsula through Melbourne to Geelong, where Chris had spent his first five Australian years, from 1955 to 1959. He was keen to meet his old friends again and to show me around. Geelong did not particularly appeal to me; however, the Great Ocean Road, along which we travelled part of the way, was another matter altogether. Geelong was an industrial town; there seemed to be one factory after another as we drove in on the main road. The town's civic centre was monotonous and uninspiring, and in the residential areas every block had a front fence or a hedge separating it clearly from the nature strip. I much preferred the open, garden-like appearance of Canberra. Had I perhaps begun to shed some of my European ways of looking and comparing?

During our first two summers in Canberra we had spent some weekends at the coast checking out places as far apart as Eden and Nowra. Several of our acquaintances owned a block of land at the coast and were planning to build or had already built a cottage there. Should we also acquire a block of land at the coast? After all, we both had steady jobs and a steady income. The thought of heading for the coast on weekends and for holidays and of planning and building our own weekend cottage held quite an appeal. Perhaps it would become more than a weekend cottage; perhaps we could live there in our far away old age? I had spent my earliest years near the sea – the Baltic Sea – and would always have a special affinity for the beach. So why not do it?

Blocks of land were for sale at Bawley Point, just a little bit out of the way for the majority of Canberrans, who mostly owned or were buying beach-side blocks immediately north and south of Batemans Bay. I do not remember now how much we paid for the piece of land, but we did not have enough cash available to buy it outright. The agent arranged for a loan and the paperwork was not as involved as it had been for our VW kombi. We would pay off the loan and then we would start planning the holiday house. That was our plan.

But that beach house was never built, never even designed. Several times a year we would pack the lawnmower into the back of the kombi and drive to Bawley Point to mow the grass on our block. A few times we stayed for the weekend, parking the car on the grassy foreshore, going for beach walks and swims, as well as tending to our piece of land.

On one such occasion, when we had just returned from our swim, a man approached. We had no idea from where because barely a house had been built in the area, and we had not met a soul at the beach. But this man was angry. Chris had stood behind the open car door and changed from his swimmers into his shorts. The man considered this to be rather rude and inconsiderate: his wife felt insulted for having to look at a naked man. Where was his wife? We had no idea. 'Bloody wogs,' the man muttered and stomped away.

After a couple of years of mowing grass on our block, we began to ask ourselves whether we really wanted to own a piece of beach-side land. Didn't we want to explore the country, get to know many different places, rather than spend every holiday and every long weekend mowing grass at the coast? We decided to sell. We did not lose any money nor did we make any on the sale. Prices for coastal real estate, however, rose quite dramatically the summer after we had sold our block. Bad luck for us! We never invested in another piece of land at the coast, even though part of me still dearly wants to live by the water.

Both Max and Hans, Chris's long-time friends from the migrant ship, had a keen interest in fishing, especially river fishing. Hans's interest, in fact, was much more than simply an interest – his enthusiasm for fishing was infectious. At times he seemed obsessed by it. So it did not take long for Chris also to develop an interest in the sport. He acquired some basic fishing gear, dug up some worms from our vegetable patch, and one Sunday the two of us went for a trial run to a place somewhere along the Queanbeyan River.

This is where I saw my first snake. Chris had walked upstream. I was on my own. I don't know where the snake had come from; my footsteps may have frightened it. I stood very still as it headed for the water. I watched its elegant movements as it glided effortlessly across to the other side. What a beautiful animal. Yet, from what I had heard, snakes were not only feared, they were loathed, and if a vehicle ever encountered one dozing on the bitumen, the honourable thing for the driver to do was to squash it beneath the tyres by repeatedly driving over it. And if you ever found a snake sunning itself in your garden, you were supposed to kill it with a spade or garden fork. Was that really so? Incidentally, Chris never caught a fish on that day.

When the men went on one of their fishing expeditions, the families usually came along: Max and Gerda's two boys and Hans and Ilse's two girls and one boy. Those children were roughly the same age. We had no children in those early days. Their favourite spot was a narrow river flat where Flea Creek, an insignificant little rivulet, flows into the Goodradigbee River, some distance downstream from the Brindabella Valley. No one else ever seemed to go there, where there were deep swimming holes, a waterfall and an abundance of trout. But the track to that river flat was rough.

We were the only ones who did not have a four-wheel drive, although our VW kombi was quite a capable vehicle. The first time we drove down the steep and rough shortcut that turns off halfway down the Brindabella Road, I closed my eyes and prayed. But the VW made it. And how would we get out? The shortcut was then not the only access road to Flea Creek; there was a track from the Brindabella Valley that more or less followed the Goodradigbee River through private property. That was the easy way; the shortcut was the thrill.

While the men were busy catching fish – and they often caught some magnificent trout – and the children played in and out of the water, the women were busy talking or preparing meals and keeping an eye on the young ones. Sometimes we would all play around the rocks and waterholes. Both Gerda and Ilse occasionally had a go at fishing, and so did the older kids, but I never developed an interest in it. Just being out in nature, soaking up the sun and sounds of the surroundings, was enough for me.

Chris's biggest catch was a four-and-a-quarter-pound trout of which he was very proud. Hans, who always knew where the biggest fish could be found, one day caught a trout that weighed almost three times that. He was so proud of it that he took it to a taxidermist and had it mounted on a board which he hung, picture-like, in his lounge room. Whether it was a pretty sight or not is debatable. Hans certainly was proud of it.

In the summer of 1967, Chris and I camped for a whole week at

Flea Creek and never saw another human being in all that time, an experience unimaginable in populated and heavily fenced Germany. It was bliss! One night, heavy rain fell after a crashing thunderstorm. The next morning all around us the forest smelled of cough lollies: the fragrance of the eucalyptus trees. For me the beauty of the place and the isolation became an unforgettable experience.

Occasionally, we spent a weekend at Flea Creek with our fishing friends. We slept in our van, the others put up their tents. At night we sat around the fire and I learned how to make billy tea, but I never developed a taste for the strong brew. Once or twice during the fishing season we would go to the Snowy Mountains to places like Ravine, camping along a peaceful mountain stream, enjoying the majestic surroundings, the sunshine and each other's company. And here, too, Hans would know where the biggest fish could be found. And he found them.

Then Max heard about another good fishing spot on the Goodradigbee, further downstream from Flea Creek, a place called McIntyre's Hut. The men were keen to go there. For our kombi, the track into the valley was definitely too rough, so we left the car at the top of the steep incline and got a lift with the others. I do not remember how the fishing went on that particular day, but I know the men were concerned about making it back up the hill with fully laden vehicles.

Max was convinced there was a track on the other side of the river from where it might be easier to get back to civilisation. He was going to try and cross the river in his Land Rover. However, he got stuck halfway through and never made it across. Hans had to winch him out bit by slow bit.

It was almost dark when we finally set off for home, Hans still giving Max's car some assistance on the very steep parts of the track, and some of us walking up the hill. Our car was waiting for us at the top, and together the three vehicles returned to Canberra. But Max's car kept stalling, and when he finally reached home the engine had given up completely. It had been an expensive day's outing for Max, but he had his Land Rover repaired and kept it for many more years and many more adventures. Like Hans, he was a bit of a mad bushman.

He must have known the Brindabellas very well, at least all the fire trails that criss-crossed the mountain range. All trails were easily accessible then; there were no locked gates. At Christmas time, Max always went into the mountains to get his Christmas tree, a beautiful European spruce. He always went alone, never prepared to take anyone along or to divulge his secret source. It was not until many years later, after we had taken up bushwalking, that we came to realise that one of the arboreta hidden away in the Brindabellas must have been the source of his Christmas trees.

We had another mad adventure with those two men and their families. It happened several years later, just before Christmas 1969, when a day trip to Flea Creek was planned. We were a family of four by then, and we still had our VW kombi. When we arrived at the short cut part way down the Brindabella Road, a ranger had parked his car in front of what was supposed to be a gate, but no longer was, just before the start of the steep downhill section. He advised us that the track was closed to vehicles. I do not remember the reason (possibly bushfire danger), but I clearly remember Hans's reaction – he was a rather excitable character. 'Then we shall walk down,' he said to the ranger, who just shrugged.

By this stage we had two children, the youngest barely eight months old, the other one four months short of three years. Altogether we were six adults and seven children. Fishing gear, swimming gear, eskies and hampers were unloaded from the vehicles, and everyone shouldered their share of the load. We even took the pusher for the smallest child. It was easy to wheel him down the hill, easy for all of us to wander down the steep track, despite all the gear. Our spirits were high. We had a lovely day at the river: we swam and splashed about, we ate and drank – only the fish had not been very cooperative on that day.

Then it was time to pack up and start the hard uphill march. It was extremely slow going. It was too difficult to push the pusher uphill with a child in it, so the infant had to be carried. Very soon the small child and then the other children complained of being hot and tired and thirsty. We had no extra water with us, we had drunk it all. The adults were hot and tired and thirsty, too, but no one said anything. This was all self-inflicted, and it had been a stupid thing to do. When we finally arrived at the cars after an interminably long uphill slog (the distance is probably not more than two kilometres), we were all totally exhausted. Luckily, someone had some spare water in their car.

Of all the places we have been to in the mountains around Canberra, Flea Creek has always had a special place in our hearts. However, it has changed considerably since then. As Canberra grew, so did the number of people visiting the area. Walkers sometimes came down there, walking in along the shortcut and out along the private river track, having arranged for a car shuttle. The private road was eventually closed and, for a while, the area became the playground of four-wheel drives and dirt bike riders whose noisy vehicles shattered the peace of the place. Now it is part of the Brindabella National Park. The shortcut road has been much improved, but it is still as steep as ever. There are proper camping and toilet facilities now, but for us it is no longer what it used to be: that sense of isolation, the feeling of being part of nature, has been irretrievably lost.

# 5

# Working – typewriters and tea ladies

By the end of August, just four weeks after our wedding and two months after arriving in this country, I had a job, and I had obtained it through connections. Chris's boss on the telecommunications project was a good friend of Mr W, the Canberra branch manager of Philips Electrical Industries. Mr W needed an office assistant to help with administrative tasks at the branch office but had been too busy to look for one, so if I could type and take shorthand, he was prepared to take me on.

The office was on the first floor of a building in Petrie Street in Civic. But it wasn't really an office; it was a store, a warehouse almost, with a couple of desks hidden among mountains of boxes. There were boxes everywhere: of fluorescent tubes, of light bulbs, of transistors, resistors and capacitors, of valves and all sorts of other electronic components, the names of which I had never heard before. The boxes were stacked right up to the high ceiling, and the storeman was forever carrying his long ladder around. Mr W had a small office, I had a desk just outside it, surrounded by boxes. It was all rather claustrophobic, but I had a job; and that was what mattered.

Staff included a Scottish storeman, named Hugh McG, the second Scot named Hugh I had met in my two months in Australia, and he had an even broader and more difficult-to-grasp accent than the first one I'd met. There was a sales representative whose task it was to canvas retailers, government departments and educational institutions in an effort to obtain orders for anything from radios and television sets to highly specialised medical equipment, all of which were delivered directly from Sydney. The Canberra branch stocked and supplied only small items and quantities. I was officially employed as a typist/stenographer, so I would take shorthand, type letters, attend to the mail and the filing, and answer the telephone. I was also expected to make tea for everyone.

I could type, I could do shorthand, even English shorthand, and I could spell, so typing letters was no big deal, not even on a manual typewriter. Letters were mostly straightforward and, to our ears today, rather stilted: 'Dear Sir, In reply to your communication of 13 inst.…' with the letter being addressed not to Mr John Brown but to John Brown Esq. (Esquire). I never typed any letters to a woman, so have no idea how she would have been addressed other than perhaps Mrs John Brown.

I was also a well-organised person, so keeping the office in order came more or less naturally; and as I was the only female in the office, I didn't see anything wrong with my having to prepare morning and afternoon tea, wash the dishes and shop for supplies. But, oh, the telephone! After only two months in the country, I still had difficulties understanding fast-speaking Australians even in a face-to-face conversation. But on the telephone! And when the speakers then rattled off their orders of items which didn't mean a thing to me: one box 40W ES (Edison screw) and two boxes 60W BC (bayonet cap) plus a certain type of resistor and a certain type of capacitor, I felt like putting the phone back on the hook and running away, never to return. But I persevered or, rather, Mr W persevered with me, because after the first week we had a little talk and he suggested that perhaps he should employ an older person for the office and I could be the junior (I was twenty-three) and learn from her. How kind of him to keep me on! Another week went by but no extra person turned up. After three weeks, Mr W said he felt we could manage without that older person. And we did!

The most exciting thing that happened during my time with Philips in Civic was the royal visit. The Queen and her Prince were on a visit to Australia, and on this particular day the royal entourage was passing through Civic. Mr W told me to go and have a look. And of course,

I did. I had seen the Queen's palace in London, and here now I saw the real Queen. I don't recall whether I was greatly impressed; perhaps I was – but maybe more by the cheering, flag-waving crowd than by the actual person at whom the cheering and flag-waving were directed.

Business was booming, and the office and storage space became ever more crammed. We needed to move to bigger premises. A new branch office building was being constructed in Wentworth Avenue in Kingston, and about a year after I started work with Philips, we moved to these much bigger, brighter and friendlier premises. There was a showroom downstairs, a large storage area at the back, Mr W had a sunny office upstairs, and my space was again next to his office, with the sales representatives' desks further along, and all was open plan and spacious, sun-drenched and air-conditioned. I even got a pay rise: from £16 to £17 a week, always paid in cash, in a neat little envelope every week. I was later to get another pay rise to £18, but that was the top of the range for my position and the work I did.

As long as the Philips branch office was located in Civic, I walked to work – a good half hour or so from Campbell. On hot or cold or rainy days, I took the bus. After the move to Kingston, I had to take the bus to work. With a bicycle, I could have cycled there, but in those days a bicycle on the road was an absolute rarity – probably a dangerous undertaking too. There was also no question of my driving the car, our VW kombi, to work. Chris needed it. He was working for an electrical contractor at various construction sites and needed the vehicle to carry his tools. No company car for him; not then anyway.

With the increase in office space came an increase in staff members and in activities. An extra sales representative came on board; a young woman – younger than I, definitely a junior – was employed to mind the showroom downstairs and to make the tea; and a service division was established. An Englishman by the name of Shad was in charge of it. He was the one with whom we became friends and whose home we were soon visiting most Friday nights, where we enjoyed the company of other young people newly arrived in town.

It was said that Mr W was one of the old guard, whatever that meant. He certainly was always Mr W to all his staff, although he was about the same age as the other men; early forties probably. He even objected to staff members using first names while on duty. I certainly felt at ease with this arrangement, because I had not yet come to terms with calling people by their first names, at least not when they were decidedly older than I or in some position of authority.

My time with Philips had certainly given me an encouraging start to the Australian employment scene. This had actually been the first proper job I ever had, apart from several casual jobs during university breaks. But eventually I felt I needed more of a challenge, so on Saturdays I started purchasing *The Canberra Times* to study the Positions Vacant column. It wasn't long before I found something that caught my imagination: the Intergovernmental Committee for European Migration (ICEM), whose headquarters were in Geneva and whose local office was in Barton, was looking for an additional staff member for a range of clerical and administrative duties. I applied, and I think the reason my application was successful was the fact that the chief of mission was a German. I was not to be his secretary, because that position was already filled. But if Mr von A ever needed something typed in German, which he occasionally did, I was at hand.

ICEM was located within the Department of Immigration, and that department was located in several temporary huts in Barton, not far from the recently filled Lake Burley Griffin. I could walk to work again, through the bushland behind Campbell which was then still undissected by Northcott Drive, across the Russell Offices complex, over Kings Avenue Bridge, and there I was. In these temporary huts, ICEM occupied four rooms, each of them roughly the size of an average living room. The chief of mission had one room; his secretary, a young Australian woman, shared hers with a long row of filing cabinets; then there was Mr Z, manager and second-in-charge, who also shared his room with a number of filing cabinets. And finally, next to his office, there was a room for the support staff: three women and their three desks complete with manual typewriters. My co-workers were a middle-aged Englishwoman by the name of Bessie, and Pat, a young Australian woman who turned out to be not just talkative but rather prone to exaggeration. The third desk was for me. I had actually exchanged a bright and airy office for another dark and cramped space. But, fortunately, this was not to last.

The Department of Immigration needed more space, and so did ICEM. So about a year after I started there, I once again moved with my employer, this time to a private residence in Red Hill. Here ICEM remained for the best part of two years before moving into proper office space in one of the new office buildings in Hobart Place, Civic. In the Red Hill house, the general staff spread out over the living/dining area, and the bosses set up their offices in the various bedrooms. By this time, we were no longer living in Campbell but in Curtin, and once again I had to use the bus to get to work.

As its name suggests, ICEM was dealing with Europeans wanting to migrate. As far as Australia and the local ICEM office were concerned, these migrants were mostly Italians and Greeks keen to come here. ICEM arranged transport for them, almost exclusively by sea, advancing interest-free loans for those eager to start a new life down under but lacking sufficient funds to pay for the voyage. These loans were to be repaid once the migrants had settled in Australia.

Not every new arrival, however, was in a position to discharge his or her debt in accordance with the contract. There were hardship cases, as there always are, but there were also a few who shunned their obligations and some who disappeared altogether. We three women, under Mr Z's supervision, had to make sure that repayments were made regularly. If they weren't, standard letter no. 1 went out. If there was no response, it was time for standard letter no. 2. If a letter was returned undelivered, letters went out to employers or neighbours in an effort to find the culprit. If correspondence failed, ICEM had two liaison officers, one based in Sydney, the other in Melbourne. We provided them with the migrant's relevant details, and they then had to go out and play detective, sometimes with success, oftentimes not. Occasionally, this would involve a trip of several days, for example to the tobacco-growing region of northeast Victoria where many single migrant men were employed.

When I joined ICEM, the staff already consisted of a mixture of nationalities: two Australians, two Germans, one Englishwoman and Mr Z, who was Polish. Later, when our workload increased and we moved to Red Hill, the staff became even more multicultural, although I am not sure if that word had been invented then. A young Polish woman, Stenia, joined us – and I am still friends with her today – as well as a young Greek girl, Fofy, who was to assist with anything pertaining to arrivals from Greece, as they often wrote in their own language and in their own script. When our chief of mission had completed his term in Australia and returned to Geneva, an Australian became the new chief of mission, a lieutenant-colonel. And when our Polish-Australian manager needed an offsider, a young Australian man, Paul, came on board. And there were occasional changes among the support staff.

How did such a motley crew get along with each other? *Did* we all get along with each other? Overall, I seem to remember, we did quite well. Our Polish-born manager had lived in England for many years before coming to Australia, and Stenia had come to Australia at such a young age that she remembered little of her first years and considered herself an Australian. I just wanted to do my job, and do it well, and hopefully fit in as best I could. Some of the friction actually originated not from us newcomers, us strangers, but from some of the true-blue Australian staff members.

One lady in particular was simply over-sensitive, I felt. Let's call her Sue. If there was any criticism of anything Australian – its food, its way of life, even its weather (and in this, young Fofy was particularly vocal) – Sue would immediately respond with 'Well, if you don't like it here, why don't you go back to where you came from?' or something along those lines. I had been told early on that Australians did not take kindly to newcomers who dared to criticise – or sometimes even just comment on – their country and their way of life. Even a comment could be taken as criticism by an overly sensitive person.

Fofy also became the recipient of a different barb from Sue because she – Fofy – used to wear the same suit and the same blouse or jumper for a whole week, and then a different outfit for the whole of the following week. Then back to the first one. One day Sue could hold her tongue no longer and asked Fofy within earshot of all of us if she had anything else to wear except those two outfits. Downcast eyes and embarrassment all around. After all, a woman who cared for her appearance was supposed to wear something different every day. If there was ever any tension between our German chief of mission and his Polish deputy, which was conceivable considering their different backgrounds and personalities, the staff were never aware of it.

And how did we all address each other? Among the women it was, of course, first names. The chief and his deputy were addressed as Mister by all of us as well as by each other, whereas they in turn would address the women by their first names, with the exception of middle-aged Bessie. When Paul joined the staff and I was to work closely with him, I finally overcame my inhibition about first names, telling myself that this man was not much older than I – in contrast to the other two males in the office – so if he called me by my first name (which he did) I would call him by his first name. But it still took some effort on my part. The lieutenant-colonel and his deputy continued to be addressed as Mister.

These were still the days of manual typewriters. Every letter had to have two carbon copies: a pink one for the chronological file and a blue one for the subject file. If you hit the wrong key or typed the wrong word, white-out had to be applied, at least on the original and, if you were conscientious enough, also on the two copies. This was often a messy and fiddly affair, because it wasn't always easy to line up the three layers of paper and the two layers of carbon paper after you had used the white-out.

Typing stencils for the Roneo machine, the forerunner of the photocopier, was another messy affair. If you mistyped, your repair fluid was a pink liquid which was used to cover up the tiny incisions or perforations made by the typewriter key; the letter or word was then typed again over the dried pink fluid. A stencil was typed without the ribbon and the perforations could, therefore, be quite drastic. In the case of the letter 'o', for example, the incision could be so thorough that the inside of the 'o' fell out and all Roneoed copies then showed every 'o' as a small black orb. The finished stencil was then attached to the drum of the duplicating machine and, if I remember correctly, every copy necessitated a turn of the drum. After the Roneo came a machine that made photostat copies, and then sometime during the 1970s 'real' photocopiers appeared in offices, although initially they were very basic compared to today's sophisticated models.

The first electric typewriters appeared in our office in the mid-1960s and most of us were a little frightened of them and took our time to get used to them. And when computers made their appearances in offices in the early 1980s, that for me was an even more frightening experience. But that is another story.

Our office hours and working conditions were those of the Public Service. Our pay was slightly higher because of the transient nature of the organisation. Upon resignation, a staff member received severance pay, which was in lieu of the public service's superannuation.

In those days, before sidewalk cafés had come into existence and before take-aways had proliferated, everyone brought their lunch to work, usually a sandwich or two. But for morning and afternoon tea breaks, we at ICEM had the services of the Department of Immigration's tea lady who, with her trolley laden with all the paraphernalia for tea making, did her rounds from room to room, once in the morning and again in the afternoon.

Once we had moved to Red Hill, to a proper house with a proper kitchen, most staff members made their own tea, except, of course, the secretary was expected to make it for the chief of mission. Whether the women then took turns washing up or it was the task of the most junior staff member, I do not recall.

I worked for ICEM until the end of February 1967, seven weeks before our first child was born. Six months after his birth, with childcare arranged, I was back, but now only on a part-time, casual and as-required basis. For perhaps a few weeks or a few months at a time, I would work on a special project that was outside the day-to-day operations of the organisation; occasionally I relieved an absent staff member. I found it easy to slip back into a still familiar office environment. And electric typewriters no longer terrified me. Eventually, this work petered out, but by then we had two children, and for a while I was a full-time mum.

Chris, meanwhile, had left the employment of the electrical contractor and, since the beginning of 1966, was working for Wormald Brothers (later Wormalds Fire Protection Co.) as a fire alarm technician. Apart from better pay and conditions, his new job provided us with two additional benefits: the use of a company car, although it was only a little Mini panel van, and a telephone installed in our Curtin home. The reason was that, as a fire alarm technician, Chris had to be on call every other week. This meant that during the on-call week he had to be contactable by phone at all times, including weekends. If the phone rang in the middle of the night because an alarm had gone off in a public building where Wormalds had installed a fire alarm system, he had to go there immediately, and if it was a false alarm – which it often was – he had to find the fault and fix it. If there was a real fire, the fire brigade was usually there before him. He suffered many a disturbed night's sleep, and so did I, because the telephone would wake me up, too, and I could never get back to sleep until Chris was safely back beside me.

There was no such thing then as a mobile phone. If we wanted to go out to a friend's home, the fire brigade had to be informed on which number Chris could be contacted during that time. During on-call weeks we could not go to the movies or to the theatre, we couldn't even have a picnic by the lake, let alone go on a walk in Canberra's nature parks. Those were the weekends we devoted to our house and our garden. Later, Chris was provided with a walkie-talkie, but its range was limited, and in any case, he was required to respond to an alarm within the shortest time possible, so had to be near a vehicle as well.

But since we had become homeowners in 1965, we had stopped going places on weekends, much preferring to stay home and work on all the big and small projects that needed to be done to turn a house into a home.

# 6

# A home of our own – bare walls and bare earth

Government housing in Canberra in the 1960s was very keenly sought after. Public servants were being transferred from Melbourne and Sydney, workers and their families came in droves, and so did migrants. They all needed a place to live. Applications for government housing were open to all residents – families, that is – of the ACT, and couples could apply even before they were married. As waiting times were close to three years, Max and Gerda encouraged Chris to put our name on the waiting list as soon as possible. They organised the application form and Chris, having no fixed address at the time other than his employer's in Sydney, gave the Lyneham address. As I had not yet left for Australia, the form was sent to me in Germany and returned immediately with my signature.

We were very modest in our expectations: a two-bedroom house would be sufficient for us: one bedroom for us, the other for the children. We would have two boys, of that I was sure; and they would naturally share a bedroom. No problem. I felt a two-bedroom house to be very generous considering where we had come from and how cramped living conditions had been in Germany for many years after the war.

There were various types of houses available, some more popular than others. If you were lucky, you were allocated the house of your choice. You were given a second and even a third chance, but if you didn't accept the third time round, you went back to the bottom of the waiting list. So it all was a bit of a gamble. Most house types were three-bedroom ones, but only one or two of them had a separate entrance hall. Usually, one walked straight into the lounge, which I have always found rather strange. We were lucky: our two-bedroom house had an entrance hall; in fact, it was virtually the same size as some of the smaller three-bedroom types.

In April 1965 we were allocated a house in Morgan Crescent, Curtin, where we still live today. 'So far out,' our friends in North and South Canberra said. 'Why would you want to move so far out? It's over the hill and in the sheep paddocks.' True, that's where it was; we had no choice, because the government houses available then happened to be in Hughes and Curtin, the first two suburbs under construction in what was to become the Woden Valley. Of course, we were eager to move out of our tiny garage-sized flat into something bigger. We were not even going to wait for a second or third chance. This was it.

We signed whatever needed signing and moved in on 1 May 1965. There wasn't much to move. A friend lent us not only his trailer but the vehicle to tow it as well. And then he was there to help shift the sofa bed, the two easy chairs, the cabinet and the radio set and our small record collection, the matching bookcase our friend Konrad had made for us in the meantime, plus the two kitchen stools and the fridge. That was all the furniture we owned. And, of course, the crate with some of my dowry still waiting to be unpacked. Clothes, books, linen, pots and pans and kitchen utensils were packed in the car. It didn't take long for it all to be unloaded and taken into the house. There was still quite a bit of empty space after the furniture had been positioned.

The house had an eat-in kitchen with several built-in cupboards, including some wall-mounted ones, all painted a pale blue. There was an electric stove. In the adjacent small laundry there was a laundry basin. We needed a washing machine. Next to the kitchen and looking over the backyard was the lounge room with a prominent Rayburn wood heater, its chimney protruding into the kitchen. The Rayburn was a wonderful and efficient heater; no matter how cold it was outside, our house was always comfortably warm.

The view out of the large lounge room window was of fences, roofs, bare earth and the Hills hoist sitting right in the middle of the backyard. It was moved into a corner and out of sight within the first few weeks. The two bedrooms were as bare as the lounge room: no built-in wardrobes, raw timber floors, a lonely light bulb in the middle of the ceiling. All walls and ceilings were painted white. All doors were painted grey and extended right up to the ceiling, which gave the whole place a rather lofty and airy appearance. There were fly screens on all windows and doors.

In the bathroom there was a bathtub with a shower head above it. Just as well we were not the types who yearned for long soaking baths, because at 1.2 metres the bathtub was nowhere near long enough to stretch out in. The hot water tank stood in one corner of the bathroom. It took sixty litres and looked anything but attractive with its pipes and metal surfaces. There was a hand basin below a high window, a tiny bathroom cupboard with a mirrored front, and then of course there was the toilet. The bathroom measured no more than 4.5 square metres. Its window had a small permanent opening with fly wire across. Why? I wondered. Apparently, the opening was there to cope with moisture and smells. Wouldn't a ceiling fan be a better idea? On winter mornings the bathroom was very cold. A ceiling fan was soon installed and the gap was closed for good. Every room in the house had in fact several ventilation grids high up on each outside wall. They might have been useful, but they were ugly and before long we covered them up with wallpaper.

What we needed most of all was a dining table, some chairs and a bed, and all three were purchased without too much ado. We also longed for a doona. Up until now we had managed English-style, with blankets. But a doona is just so much more cosy and warming. Doonas then were a rarity, but we persevered and eventually found one. A wardrobe? We wanted built-in ones as the necessary space was there, but other things were more urgent. As we did not want to go into debt for items that were not absolutely necessary, Chris constructed a metal frame which functioned as a wardrobe, until we had the money and our cabinetmaker friend Konrad had the time to make built-in wardrobes for the two bedrooms. Clothing like jumpers, socks and underwear normally stored in a chest of drawers had to stay in a suitcase or in the wooden chest in which I had brought my dowry.

At least now there was enough space in the kitchen cupboards to accommodate the dinner set and the cutlery, the Japanese tea set and other little treasures. The lounge room looked rather bare for a while with only the sofa bed, two easy chairs, a bookcase and the radio cabinet. For a coffee table we used another wooden chest that Chris owned, wrapped a tablecloth around it, put an ashtray on top and a coffee table book, and the lounge already looked friendlier. A sturdy carton with, again, a tablecloth wrapped around it, functioned as a stand for our collection of cacti.

Nothing for the house was acquired on lay-by or on hire purchase. If we did not have the money to pay for it outright, we went without it until we had saved up sufficient dollars. That was how we had been brought up. And so the furnishing of our house proceeded only very gradually.

Sitting at the kitchen table with my sewing machine after work or on weekends, I set about making curtains for the various rooms while Chris made the pelmets. We also invested in light fittings, because a room with a single bulb in the middle of the ceiling was a rather bleak sight. We acquired a second-hand washing machine: a twin-tub with a wringer on top – still a long way away from a fully automatic one. That would have to wait a couple more years; when the children came along it would really be needed.

Another household item – thought of as indispensable today and which we did not acquire for a number of years – was a television set. We had our radio, we had records and books, and that was enough entertainment. Besides, if you owned a television, a licence fee was payable, a fee that also included your radio. But if you only had a radio, would anybody worry if it wasn't licensed? We didn't ask.

But back to the new house and its interior. What were the floors like? They were just bare, untreated timber, radiata pine, rather pale and knotty in places, but interesting-looking. They needed immediate attention. Polished timber flooring was not the fashion at the time. Carpets were, and colourful and heavily patterned ones at that, but we had had polished floorboards in Germany with rugs to soften the impact, and that was what we wanted to have now too. Furthermore, carpets were costly; the polishing could be a do-it-yourself job. Each night after work, each weekend, Chris was down on his knees with yet another sheet of coarse sandpaper sanding yet another part of the room, until all three rooms and the hallway were sanded down. No one we knew owned a sander, and to hire one over several weeks would have been too costly. When the sanding was finished, several coats of Estapol were applied, and so one room after another began to look fresh and bright.

The kitchen was the only room where the bare floorboards were covered with a soft-backed type of linoleum. Eventually, once we had warmed to the idea of wall-to-wall carpet, we followed that trend, too. And then, many years (no, decades) later – in fact, not until the end of the 1900s – the carpets were ripped up and the floors once again polished; this time, however, proper timber floorboards were laid on top of the radiata pine, giving the place a modern look.

Here I am talking about our house, when in fact initially it wasn't ours at all. We rented it. But we could apply to purchase it, the rules said, and the process should not take longer than six months. We applied very soon after moving in. Before that we had investigated purchasing an established house in one of Canberra's older suburbs like Kingston or Manuka. The real estate agent virtually talked us out of it: the deposit would be high, the interest rate as well, and the repayments might be hard for us to meet if we didn't have a sizeable deposit. Which we did not, but we both had steady jobs. 'But what if you decide to have a family,' the agent said, 'and only one income? Apart from that,' he continued, 'you'll probably have difficulty getting a loan in the first place.'

The government, however, made it easy for us to purchase the house. Their conditions were 5% deposit, the balance payable over forty-five years – yes, forty-five years – at an interest rate of 5.75% fixed, with a rebate of 1% if payments were made by the due date; therefore, effectively an interest rate of 4.75%. Forty-five years sounded a horrendously long time to us. It would take us all the way to 2010. Would we still be around then? Yes, even that question crossed our minds. But we were encouraged from all sorts of quarters and so we took the leap. We scraped our last dollars together in order to pay more than the required 5% deposit. But the clerk at the housing office wouldn't accept any more than the minimum deposit. 'Take the balance home, dear,' he said to me, 'and use it to buy furniture. It won't make any difference over the long term.' How right he was, and what a sensible piece of advice! So, as of 19 August 1965, the house was ours, with a purchase price of £4,487 ($8,964). We had only lived in it just over three and a half months.

Repayments were £19.2.9 a month, about $39 and a few cents, over the next forty-five years. By the 1980s, when Paul Keating was treasurer, we still owed a couple of thousand dollars on the loan. Interest rates were extremely high at the time and, even though we had spare money by then, it was wiser to invest that than to pay off the loan. Keating, however, had his eyes on the thousands of Canberrans who, like us, enjoyed cheap housing loans while the rest of the population was groaning under the burden of high interest rates. He proposed to adjust our mortgages to bring them in line with those of other home buyers, but there was such a public outcry that the proposal was soon scrapped. Nonetheless, we increased our monthly payments and on 16 August 1994 we had paid off our house. It had taken twenty-nine years.

Of course, the house eventually proved too small for a family of four, so there were a number of additions and alterations. The first addition – a larger lounge – was started as early as the summer of 1967, less than eighteen months after we had purchased the house. Chris's mother had passed away in Germany, and he inherited some money – just enough to pay for the extension. Another addition – a master bedroom with an en suite – followed ten years later, while minor alterations and various other improvements were carried out in a somewhat haphazard fashion over the years.

The house, with its roughly one-hundred square metres, was an absolutely bare bones house when we moved in, but the exciting thing was that all that empty space was ours to fill, ours to furnish, to live in and to enjoy. We were happy.

Just as the size of the house was modest, so was the size of the block. Peering over the wooden fences into our neighbours' backyards and comparing the spaces at the front of the houses, we were convinced that all the neighbours had bigger blocks of land; but then again, they all had three-bedroom houses. We were a bit disappointed, because we were planning a large vegetable garden, flowers bed, fruit trees, other trees and shrubs. Where would it all fit? Years later, we didn't mind the smaller block: less lawn to mow, less garden to maintain, less work.

And just as the house was bare bones, so was the piece of land that surrounded it: nothing but bare earth, not a single tree on it, no shrub, not even a blade of grass, except some weeds. Every block around us looked the same. Two narrow concrete strips ran from the street to the gate, that was the driveway, and another concrete strip ran from the driveway to the front door. The rest of the space, all that bare earth, was again ours to do with as we pleased, to design it, to sow and plant, and to enjoy it. It was all very exciting! Never mind the hard work. Our friends in old Canberra were right: we had moved to what had formerly been sheep paddocks. But we didn't care.

After consulting friends and *The Canberra Gardener* and talking to neighbours, the appropriate lawn seed was decided upon, and the whole front garden initially became lawn. Trees and shrubs would be planted later around the periphery. A gum tree was planted on our nature strip by what is now City Parks, and we were thrilled about that. A bit of the bush right at the front door! We watered the tree along with our lawn and it grew rapidly. Unfortunately and stupidly, it had been planted directly under the power lines, and once it was within reach of those wires, it had to go. That was very sad for us at the time, but now we are happy that we do not have such a giant in our garden. Our neighbour, who was not fond of gum trees and did not want one on his nature strip, simply pulled it out a few weeks after it had been planted.

As Canberra was to be a garden city, the government – at that time, long before self-government, we were under the watchful eye of the Department of the Interior – had decided that every new home in Canberra would be entitled to a free issue of trees and shrubs from its nursery in Yarralumla: up to ten trees and up to forty shrubs per house, all of them natives. We were provided with a long list of suitable plants to choose from and studied it carefully as we were not at all familiar with the native flora. We chose to the best of our ability and eventually took delivery of them (but not the full complement) once our front lawn was reasonably well established. Of course, the garden also had to have a touch of home: so apart from the native shrubs, there were roses, dahlias and gladioli. And three birch trees!

Of course, we did not want any weeds to spoil that perfect-lawn look. So, while the lawn was still young, we would spend several hours on weekends pulling out every tiny bit of weed that threatened our future perfect lawn. The enthusiasm for pulling out weeds lasted perhaps two summers, then the clover came in and the couch grass, and now, nearly fifty years down the track, we barely have a lawn left because of the scarcity of water and its costs.

In the back garden, different things were happening. First of all, there was concreting to be done. We had a metal garage put up, and the concrete strips that finished at the gate had to be extended to the garage door. Other concrete paths had to be put in along the back wall of the house and around what was going to be our vegetable patch. The rest of the backyard would be lawn with shrubs along the side fences, and berry bushes along the back fence, with fruit trees suitably spaced in the grassy areas: apricot, peach, cherry, apple. What a wonderfully productive garden this was going to be!

The vegetable patch was a neat rectangle of some two metres by five. Raked paths divided neat beds and plantings were plentiful: carrots and cabbage, peas and pumpkin, radishes and rhubarb – it was all there and it was growing well. At least initially. Over the years, the grubs and insects arrived and the various diseases, black spot and brown rot and cabbage flies and aphids by the millions. The need for more and more spraying became more and more pressing, and in the end we capitulated; the fruit trees disappeared one after the other, and the vegetable patch was eventually turned into lawn. Apart from that, the carrots and cabbages one bought at the markets were so much bigger than anything we had ever grown. Today the trend is back to growing your own vegetables, and we again have a vegetable patch, but only a very small one, mainly for growing herbs.

As far as the concrete went, it was all of the home-made variety – that is, we bought sand and gravel and cement and a wheelbarrow in which the mixture was moistened and mixed. So wheelbarrow by wheelbarrow our various garden paths were being constructed. All this work we did by ourselves. This is how we now spent our weekends: no more fishing trips to Flea Creek or trips to the coast, no more Sunday strolls or visits to friends. Often we hoped that friends would not suddenly turn up uninvited and interrupt our concreting, planting and weeding. That's how obsessed we were with the work to be done.

Not only did the government give us trees and shrubs at no cost, in those early days every householder also received an annual free allocation of water. After all, we were expected to keep our nature strips green, and they were, in reality, not our responsibility but the government's. We did the watering for them. Yes, water was cheap and plentiful at the time, or in any case, we did not worry about wastage like sprinkler run-off into the gutter, washing the car in the driveway or hosing down all those concrete paths. For that matter, sprinklers, whether manual or automatic, would often run in the middle of the day, even when hot northerlies were blowing. And in autumn, when the leaves were falling, there were little fires smouldering in many gutters, as people burnt the leaves, a practice which has long been disallowed. When winter came, on many a Sunday we headed for the mountains. In true do-it-yourself fashion, we went to the Brindabellas to collect firewood; there was so much around and I don't think that collecting it was illegal then. But we never took a chainsaw, because we never owned one.

When our house looked reasonably presentable, we had a housewarming party to which we invited everyone we had come to know over the past three years: German-speaking people and English-speaking ones. The only worry was visitors with high heels, stiletto heels, which were very fashionable then and which could easily put dents into the timber flooring No one would have dreamed of asking their guests to take their shoes off, as is often the case today.

Now that we were living in our own home, away in the paddocks in the new suburb of Curtin, we learned a few more things about the Australian way of life that we had been unaware of while staying in our little backyard flat in Campbell. The milkman came around every evening, noisily delivering as many full bottles of milk as empty ones had been left out. There virtually was only one kind of milk. Once a week, or perhaps a fortnight, the milkman left his bill with the bottles and cash was left out in return. Once the cash began to disappear here and there, customers paid their milkman by cheque. And eventually the milkman discontinued his services altogether.

Bread was delivered early in the mornings so that everyone had a fresh loaf of bread for breakfast. The system worked on a similar basis to that of the milkman. We never made use of it, though, because the white and doughy stuff that was on offer was not what we liked, and I think that was the only type of bread that was delivered. Bread deliveries went the same way as milk deliveries: they were actually the first ones to disappear.

In the spring of 1967 the supermarket in Curtin opened. Other, smaller shops had already established themselves there: a greengrocer, a butcher, a milk bar, a barber and a hairdresser. But now, here was a big supermarket with rows and rows of goods on offer. Such a variety as we had rarely seen before, now almost on our doorstep. Such a choice! Some years later, the first supermarket opened in the Woden Plaza, now Westfield Shopping Town. My neighbour – always one for a bargain – told me that the Woden supermarket was truly cavernous, but did not necessarily offer a bigger choice, just more of everything. Since then, the choices and varieties of all that can be found on supermarket shelves have increased tremendously to the point where choosing between brands and types and flavours has become a rather irritating and sometimes even stressful task.

In those days it certainly was a more honest and a more trusting society. We were told that many people never locked their back doors. Max and Gerda never did. We did, but would often forget to close a window when we went out. Nothing ever happened. Years later, after we had experienced several burglaries, we became much less trusting and much more security conscious. Today we have security screens and security doors, but how secure are we really?

Since Chris had started with Wormalds in early 1966, we'd had a telephone, but overseas calls were still out of the question. They remained prohibitively expensive for many years to come. When Chris's father died in 1967, we received no phone call, not even a telegram. By the time the letter arrived notifying us of his passing, the funeral had already taken place. And when our children were born, family and friends overseas were similarly advised by letter.

The postman did his rounds twice a day on his bicycle; and every time he dropped an item into your letter box, he blew his whistle to let you know that he had been. The bicycle soon made way for a small postie motorbike, and the twice-daily mail deliveries did not last very much longer either. If, for some reason, you had put insufficient stamps on your envelope, a card from the post office would arrive in your letter box asking for the shortage to be made up by fixing stamps to the card and returning it. In the meantime, the card pointed out, the post office had been so kind as to forward your letter anyway, so please be so kind in return and pay your debt.

Because Curtin and Hughes, then the only two Woden Valley suburbs, were more or less surrounded by paddocks with a bit of an arboretum at its north-western fringe, the bush flies were a great pest during the summer months. And so were the mosquitoes. The bush flies have long disappeared, but not so the mozzies. On still and balmy summer evenings, there was another unpleasantness, the smell from the Weston Creek sewerage works. Luckily, they were relocated within a year or so of our move to Curtin.

On a Saturday in July 1965, while Chris was at work and I was doing my housewifely duties at home, it started to snow. The world outside was grey and still, the clouds were low, snowflakes were drifting to earth and in the course of the day were covering the ground. What a wonderful white world it was! It felt like Christmas to me. I was humming Christmas carols and was ready to bake gingerbread biscuits, but I didn't have all the ingredients. I had no car and the nearest shop for those sorts of ingredients would have been in Civic. The next day the snow was gone, but the following winter there was another day of snowfall and the world outside again was white and Christmassy-looking for a short time.

# 7

# And then we were four – nappies flapping in the wind

The Pill was on the market when we married. Suddenly women had a real choice about not simply when, but even if, they wanted to have children. There was never any doubt in my mind that we would have children – remember, I was planning on two boys – but if at all possible I did not want them right away. Our living quarters would have been much too cramped, but we also wanted to get on our feet first, to have a proper home and some money in the bank. So every night I popped a pill, and every six months I went to the doctor for a check-up and a new prescription. When I was twenty-seven, four years into our marriage, the doctor reminded me that if we wanted children, it would be a good idea to give up the Pill now, otherwise I would be too old for a first-time mother. So I gave it away.

On 18 April 1967, our son Tim Christopher was born at Royal Canberra Hospital, the one by the lake that disappeared in a botched implosion some thirty years later to make room for the National Museum of Australia. He weighed 3,500 grams and was fifty-one centimetres long. It was an easy pregnancy, no morning sickness, no sleepless nights, only the occasional backache during the last few weeks. I worked till seven weeks before the due date; there was no problem with my employer.

Shortly before the birth, in early April, I accompanied Chris on a work trip in his Mini panel van to the Snowy Mountains. He had to service fire alarms in various ski lodges in Perisher. After the work was done, we continued up along the Kosciuszko Road right to the very top of Australia's highest mountain. A large section of the road was still unsealed and the final bit, from Rawson's Pass, was particularly rough, but the Mini made it to the top. And there I finally stood, close to nine months pregnant, under the summit trig, and looked out over a mountainous landscape that seemed to run to infinity. Although the Australian Alps were nothing like their Swiss namesake or even their New Zealand counterparts, they had a charm all their own; they were gentler in appearance, mellowed with age perhaps.

During the pregnancy, I turned up once a month at the doctor's surgery for a check-up and to be weighed and have my blood pressure taken. Towards the end I had to show up once a week for a more thorough check-up. That was all. No other tests were carried out, perhaps not even available, definitely not to a healthy pregnant woman.

As a first-time mother, my moods during the nine-month wait vacillated between elation and anxiety. There were times when I really worried, not simply whether and how I would cope with the birth and with a newborn, but also about the type of world this baby would be born into, what sort of future it would face. I did not want our child – or our children – to ever have to experience war. Surely, Australia was far enough away from all the possible theatres of war?

The doctor had calculated the due date as 18 April, a Tuesday. That was the date our child was going to be born, whether he/she was ready for it or not. I had to report to the hospital early that morning. Chris took me and stayed until all preliminaries were completed and I was assigned a hospital bed. Encouraged by our doctor, he wanted to be with me during the birth, although it was still a rarity for other than hospital staff to be present at births. It must have been eight-thirty, perhaps nine o'clock, the time of day when people go to work. I told Chris labour would take hours – that's what we had been told at the prenatal classes I had conscientiously attended. There we expectant mothers had been taught all manner of things about the actual birth as well as various exercises, in particular how to breathe properly to relax and then how to breathe and push. Later, in hospital, after the birth, we were shown how to hold and bathe a newborn, how to change its nappies, to dress and wrap it.

As the labour was apparently going to take a long time, I suggested to Chris that he might as well go to the office, organise his day and come back in due course. When he did come back, not more than three hours later, there was Tim all wrapped up and sound asleep in a little cot by my side. I remember little of the birth itself, only that, as labour started, I was asked if I would allow several trainee nurses to watch the process. I barely noticed their presence; I was too occupied with breathing and pushing. These were still the days when a newborn was briefly held upside down, given a little slap until he/she cried, then washed, wrapped up and put into a cot. The cot was then wheeled next to the mother's bed, and finally the mother could at least have a look at her newborn. If it was asleep, she couldn't hold it until it had woken up. At night all babies were wheeled into a separate room so that the mothers could get some uninterrupted sleep.

I stayed in hospital for a week, which was the norm at the time, certainly enough time to get some rest, gain confidence in handling a newborn and even to get to know some of the women with whom I shared a room. One woman had been in labour for twenty-four hours; another, Diana, was intending to go back to work in six weeks' time and kept mulling over her baby-minding options, of which there were barely any at the time; and a third woman came from Curtin. Our boys later went to school together.

When Chris collected us from the hospital, I held Tim in my arms; that was how you took your baby home. When we later travelled somewhere with the newborn, the bassinet would rest on the back seat of the car. It wasn't strapped in. And there still were no seat belts for driver or passenger.

There was financial assistance from the government for new families: the so-called maternity allowance, a one-off payment of $30 for the first child and $32 for the second. The money was paid immediately after birth; a $20 advance was also an option. There was also child endowment payable to the mother: fifty cents a week for the first child, $1 for the second and $1.50 for the third and subsequent children, payable until the age of sixteen or, in the case of full-time students, until age twenty-one.

We used the maternity allowance to buy a cot. A bassinet had been borrowed from friends, and all the other baby things, mainly nappies, I had purchased during the past few weeks. A big parcel had come from my mother with little jackets and jumpsuits, even German nappies that were folded and fastened around the small body in a special way and – in contrast to Australian nappies – did not need a special safety pin for fastening. Now Velcro does the job, and disposable nappies seem to have taken over. Nappies then were soaked in a special disinfectant solution in a lidded nappy bucket, and every few days the washing machine would be put to work. What a sight – a Hills hoist full of nappies flapping in the breeze.

When Tim was a few months old, we bought a collapsible pram. We also had a bouncinette and, once he could stand up, there was a playpen, borrowed from friends. When he was ready to eat his meals at the table with us, we acquired a second-hand high chair; and for the car there was a simple child's seat the 'arms' of which were slipped over the rear backrest. The infant was not fastened in the seat, nor was the seat secured in any way. We had no baby capsule or child restraint – it was not a requirement; in fact, those things may not even have existed then.

Like most first-time parents we were quite besotted with our little boy. He was bathed every morning and, according to the prevailing custom, was supposed to be breastfed every four hours, although my doctor – the mother of six – suggested that it would be much better to feed on demand. Which is what I did, and before long the child slept through the best part of the night.

Soon after I came home from hospital, a close friend of ours, a Finnish woman named Moya, who was doing her nursing training at the Royal Canberra Hospital, came over to celebrate. Chris got the champagne out and I drank a glass. Some time later I fed Tim. He slept the whole night through. But we did not repeat the exercise.

At regular intervals I took Tim to the baby health centre in Curtin, where he was weighed, measured and vaccinated according to the prescribed schedule. Everything proceeded normally.

I often thought of Diane, who was intending to return to work full-time as soon as her baby was six weeks old. I looked at Tim and decided I could not do that, definitely not at six weeks of age and definitely not full-time. But I did want to go back to work. I wanted to save up to go to Germany the following year. Also, once I had established a routine with Tim and done all the housework I possibly could, there was nothing more to do. Something was lacking.

Almost all our neighbours were families with young children and none of the mothers went to work. In one case, the husband had even forbidden his wife to go to work; he made enough money, he maintained, to provide for a family, he did not need a working wife. Pretty drastic, but she obeyed, at least for the time being. I believe she eventually found herself a part-time job when her children were at school. Some men apparently felt threatened by an independent partner, someone who had her own income. Public opinion, too, did not approve of working mothers, speaking of neglect and the possibility of bringing up delinquent children, thus instilling feelings of doubt and guilt into any mother who defied public opinion.

It certainly was not an easy time for women who, during the war years and immediately afterwards, had managed on their own, done what needed to be done and got on with life. Now they were once again to be shunted home to kids and kitchen. In the public service, for example, women had to resign their permanent position (if they had one) and become casual employees once they married. Women were not allowed to be bank tellers, just in case there was a robbery, it was said. Were men eager to protect women or their own jobs? I sometimes wondered.

There were, of course, possibilities to occupy young mothers outside the home; they could play tennis, for example, or learn a hobby, even go to university. It wasn't as if we were confined to boredom. I recall that at one time the Woden Plaza ran a bed-making competition! Can you imagine? But no matter what young mothers wanted to do for diversion, the question always was what to do with the baby. Some occasional care was available in Civic, the emphasis being on occasional, and it was needs-based. Perhaps a neighbour might help out. The odd commercially operated childcare centre had sprung up. A grandmother would have been ideal. We didn't have one here, nor did many young Australian mothers who had left their families behind in Melbourne or Sydney when their husbands had been transferred to Canberra for work.

I took Tim for walks along the near-deserted streets of Curtin in the new pram. It was always very quiet during the day with the men at work and the children at school. Occasionally I joined some of the neighbourhood women for morning or afternoon coffee or invited them to our house. I sewed and knitted; I read books and wrote letters and, of course, attended to my domestic duties.

When the supermarket opened at Curtin, there was such a large crowd milling around that it would have been impossible to take the pram into the store. As Tim was sound asleep and I was reluctant to wake him, I parked the pram outside the main entrance and plunged into the crowd in search of specials. When I came out some time later, there was a woman, a stranger, rocking the pram. The baby had woken and was crying; the rocking seemed to calm him. Had I been careless? Or trusting?

As already mentioned, by the time Tim was six months old I went back to work, but on a casual basis only, which was an arrangement that suited me very well. ICEM had by then moved to Civic, to the seventh floor of an office building in Hobart Place. I found a babysitter, too, an English woman called Margaret, mother of four, the youngest four years old, who lived in the neighbourhood, in the cul-de-sac behind us. My neighbour knew her and spoke well of her. There was no such thing as an accredited day mother. It was simply a matter of trust. On the days I went to work, I dropped Tim off at her place and drove to

Civic in the kombi. I am still amazed that I was disciplined enough to walk up those seven flights of stairs instead of taking the lift, most days anyway.

When that work temporarily petered out, we were ready for child number two.

Our son Ralph Peter was born on 22 May 1969, also at Royal Canberra Hospital. He weighed 3,350 grams and measured fifty centimetres, only a fraction smaller than his brother. This pregnancy had been almost as uneventful as my first, with one exception: for most of the first three months I suffered from morning sickness, except that it did not occur in the mornings, but in the evenings, after work, when it was time to prepare dinner. I couldn't stand the smell of food, so Chris was cooking the evening meal, which I then often couldn't eat.

Ralph was two weeks early according to the doctor's calculations, and he came into this world in a hurry. I had gone to the Curtin shops after Chris had come home from work, just to pick up a few groceries, when I felt my insides cramping up, a vaguely familiar sensation. No, this couldn't be it, not yet. It was far too early. It must be a false alarm.

I finished my shopping and went home. Chris was preparing dinner. I went to lie down. The cramps became more frequent. Chris phoned the doctor at home. Only her husband, a scientist, was there. His wife was at a meeting at the hospital. His advice to Chris was 'If I were you, I'd take my wife at once.' He should know, being the father of six children.

Into the kombi and off we rushed to hospital. At one point I feared the birth would happen in the vehicle, somewhere along Commonwealth Avenue. But we managed to get to the hospital. There was no time for any preparations. I was led to a bed at once and the doctor came rushing down the corridor from her meeting. Chris was left at reception to provide the necessary personal details. By the time that was done, Ralph was born. So even this time round Chris did not have the opportunity to be present at the birth. The post-birth procedure was still the same as it had been two years earlier. When

Chris came in, Ralph was in his cot near my bed, all cleaned and wrapped up; but he wasn't sleeping, his eyes were wide open and his head turned towards our voices. This kid was well and truly ready to face the world, we thought.

Again I was in hospital for a week while Chris stayed at home with Tim. In fact, when we rushed off to hospital on the evening of 22 May, Tim was already asleep, and we had just left him there. In all our hurry we had even forgotten to alert the neighbours. Fortunately, he was still sound asleep when Chris returned.

And now there were four of us. Because things are not as intimidating the second time round, I felt more at ease with this child. With Tim, I had persevered with breastfeeding for several months; Ralph was put straight on to the bottle. Several of my women friends had suggested that it would be much simpler that way. Later I wondered whether it really was.

Even though I felt more at ease with the new baby, he worried us for a while, because at only a few weeks of age, he would cry every evening around dinner time. If he was picked up and held or walked around, he stopped. No sooner was he put back into the bassinet than he started to cry again and no amount of rocking the bassinet would help. He wanted to be picked up. 'Watch out,' my neighbour said. 'You mustn't spoil him, otherwise you'll be forever holding him. He's imposing his will on you, the little brat.' Oh, dear! What were we to do? We tried a compromise by letting him cry a little longer and shortening the holding time. Eventually, after several weeks it seemed to work, but it was an agonising time for all of us. Today we would just hold him until he stopped crying, but things were different forty-odd years ago. We didn't want to raise a spoiled child.

It was later that same year when someone lent me a copy of Dr Benjamin Spock's book *Baby and Childcare*, the modern mother's bible of child-rearing. I had heard about it and was eager to read it. At long last here would be the guidance I had been seeking; here would be the answers to all my questions and insecurities concerning the bringing up of children. But the more I read, the more my heart sank. I had already made so many mistakes, had not been following modern methods, had been old-fashioned and had treated my children similar to the way we ourselves had been treated as children (with the exception that we always had more time for our children than our hard-working parents ever had for us). I was repeating many of the mistakes of old. This realisation weighed heavily on my mind. What could I do? How could I reverse my mistakes? Until one day I realised that the most important thing in child-rearing was to love your kids, and that I wholeheartedly did. I would love them, and as far as anything else was concerned, I would do the best I could. We both would. I gave Dr Spock's bible back to the lender. It had come too late for me.

I taught our children the nursery rhymes I remembered from my own childhood. I also told them some of the German fairy tales that I remembered, particularly the grisly ones by the Brothers Grimm which had been my staple as a child. I don't think the boys liked them very much; they preferred the much gentler English children's books, in particular those silly Dr Seuss ones. We became acquainted with those through our child-minder Margaret as well as through various babysitters and later, of course, through preschool. Gradually, the German nursery rhymes and fairy tales were replaced by English ones.

I don't think our children had many toys in their very early years: a teddy bear for sure, another soft toy, building blocks, a ball, bucket and spade for the beach. And books, definitely. One of Ralph's favourite places for playing was in front of the kitchen cupboard that held the pots and pans. He would drag them out, try to match up the various lids, use a wooden spoon to create noise. Another favourite spot of his was on top of the kitchen bench next to the stove when I was cooking. He loved to watch and, even more, to stir the pot. How dangerous that sounds to me now as I write this, but at the time it felt perfectly natural.

Life with two small children was more than double the effort of one, and despite feeling relatively at ease with the second child, I was often tired, exhausted, even frustrated by sometimes conflicting demands. Fortunately, the boys were never really very sick, apart from the usual childhood illnesses. For convenience, we had changed to a doctor in Curtin, and this doctor still made house calls if a child was ill.

With one small child we still went camping occasionally. With two small but growing children, going camping in the VW kombi van became more complicated. We still kept the vehicle for a few years, but gave away camping for a little while. Now, when we went for a drive, the kids sat on the mattresses in the back, unsecured, often playing this or that. On one never-to-be-forgotten occasion, I was driving along Commonwealth Avenue into Civic with the kids mucking around in the back. Ralph slipped off the seat and grabbed the door handle. The door flung open. I don't remember what he hung on to, but hang on he did – for dear life. All I could do in my shock and horror was drive on to the median strip and wait until we had all recovered our equilibrium. I think I took the longest. Not long after that incident, the kombi made way for a normal car.

In order to get out of the house from time to time, I attended a hobby or language course in the evenings when Chris was home to mind the children. Things became more difficult if we both wanted to go out together. This was when I became aware of the babysitting club operating in Curtin: a dozen or so families had banded together to babysit for each other, with a liaison person keeping the books. It was a very simple system and may still be in use today. When I babysat for someone, I received a credit; when someone babysat for us, we were debited. Most children were quite young, no more than preschool age, and usually in bed or ready for it when the babysitter arrived. One family had slightly older children and one boy, aged twelve, was a bit of a pain, because he thought himself an adult.

After a number of years in the babysitting club, and after I had regular part-time work, it was easier to pay a babysitter than have to stay up late on a Saturday night at someone else's house. Occasionally we would fetch Max and Gerda's sons from Lyneham to babysit our boys. Henry and Mark were teenagers then and our boys loved having them around for an evening. But once Henry was old enough to prefer going out with girls to babysitting ten-year-olds, we reverted to paying a babysitter. Until Ralph one evening suggested that they would quite happily stay at home by themselves, no babysitter needed, provided we paid them instead of a babysitter. The first time we tried this, we only went to a friend's house a few suburbs away and were easily contactable by telephone. Ralph rang up at least four times that evening; initially, I think, to ensure that we really were where we said we would be, later to complain that his older brother wouldn't let him watch a particular program on TV, and did he really have to go to bed when Tim told him to?

I went back to work when Ralph was about a year old; still with my last employer (ICEM) and still on a part-time, casual and as-required basis. Initially, both boys were minded by a woman in our street, Lorna, who had two boys the same age as ours. Margaret felt it was too much to mind both our boys. But Lorna soon felt the same and was only prepared to mind Ralph. By that time there was a fully established childcare centre in Curtin, and that is where Tim went for a while. He says his only memory of this time is that all the children had to have a midday sleep; but he never wanted to sleep in the middle of the day, he just lay there waiting for the time to pass.

Then the day came when he was due for preschool: three half-days a week. After his experience at the childcare centre, he was quite eager to go.

What he did not want to do a year later was to go to a real school. He resisted as hard as he could. I took him up to the steps leading to his classroom. His teacher, Mrs S, welcomed him at the door and was going to take his hand. Tim refused. I gave him a gentle push, he dug his heels against the steps and both Mrs S and I used all our strength to get him inside the classroom door. Mrs S told me later that Tim was fine once the door had closed behind him. I was not so sure about my own feelings.

When Ralph's turn came to go to school, he couldn't wait. He had been keen to go to preschool and he was equally keen to go to primary school. All of a sudden, there I was childless, at least for a good part of each day. I clearly remember the first time I went shopping on my own: there was no small hand for me to hold, no straying dawdler anywhere behind me. I kept waiting for that child's hand to grab mine, but it was no longer there. I felt a mixture of loss and liberation. I had always been keen for our kids to make progress. I couldn't wait for them to walk, to talk, to ride a bike, to go to school. And suddenly – and it did seem sudden now – they had begun to move away from me, to become their own little persons. They did not need me all day, every day any more. There it was: both loss and liberation.

I also clearly remember the first time I went to the movies in the middle of the day: how totally frivolous I felt. This was a luxury, and luxuries were only supposed to be indulged in once all the work was done, or perhaps on Sundays. My parents' work ethic!

Since our wedding, we had never been back inside a church, and there was never a question whether our children should be christened. It was never an issue, never talked about, until Tim was in his third or fourth year of primary school when he came home one day and wanted to know if he had been christened. When my answer was negative, he burst into tears. 'But then I can't get married in a church,' he cried. I assured him that by the time he was ready to be married, things were bound to be different and, if not, there were ways around it; in time he could make his own decision. After that, Tim no longer attended religious classes – he proudly carried a note from his parents that in future he be excused from those classes. He was apparently not the only one by a long way.

School – what was it like for our boys, being the children of migrants, of New Australians, as we were often called then? Were they hassled in any way? Were they made to feel different? Did they feel different? Tim says not much, because in the early 1970s migrant kids were no longer a rarity at schools, and with classmates who had surnames like Fenyvesi, Bulthuis and Bartholomeusz, to have Acker for a surname was not really unusual, although the name lent itself to all sorts of allusions. After all, the school held an International Day each year for which the pupils were encouraged to wear national dress. Tim went in lederhosen (leather pants) and one or two girls turned up in dirndls and the like.

What he really didn't like was the fact that his parents never had any white bread in the house. He always had to take brown bread sandwiches to school, and only about twice a year was he allowed to buy lunch from the tuck shop. He would have died for a white bread sandwich, no matter what the filling, he told me many years later. But he never got it. Were we cruel parents? Or just not sensitive enough?

The school our boys attended was North Curtin Primary. The suburb of Curtin was so full of young families, it needed two primary schools, one in the north, the other in the south. As the children grew up, went to high school and then college, the number of school-age children in Curtin declined considerably. One school, South Curtin, was closed; North Curtin remained open. Later, South Curtin was reopened and North Curtin now houses a number of community organisations.

What was new to us was that public schools were not the only schools around; our neighbour's children attended a Catholic school, of which there were a number in Canberra. Then there were the grammar schools, which were very popular with the well-to-do. In Germany everyone went to a public school; there were no church schools, and boarding schools were few and far between and really only of interest to well-heeled parents with academically not over-endowed children. At least that's how it was fifty or sixty years ago.

What was new to us as parents, too, was the extent of parental involvement in the running of the school. My parents – and Chris's even less, because he went to school during the war and the immediate post-war years – rarely attended a parent/teacher night and never a meeting of the P&C, let alone volunteer to help with various school activities. We here involved ourselves only at the margins: we attended the parent/teacher evenings, I went to the P&C meetings when I wasn't working, and at some stage I even volunteered with some craft activities in Ralph's class.

School uniforms were another novelty for us, but one we wholeheartedly agreed with. From my mother I had inherited a knitting machine, so for years I knitted the boys' grey school jumpers. Other uniform items – shorts, shirts and so on – could often be acquired second-hand at a special sale at the school.

Voluntary contributions to the running of the school were also unknown to us. In our schooldays, in Germany, we were simply given a list of required books which in the immediate post-war years had not been overly long; exercise books and writing utensils were bought as needed. What else was there that required funds? If there was a school excursion, the parents paid. If they couldn't pay, the kid didn't go. Craft? What little there was taught, the school provided the materials. Sport? The same.

Another novelty for us was the tuck shop, which was staffed by volunteering mothers. I must admit, I never volunteered and, as already mentioned, our kids were rarely ever allowed to purchase anything there. But we did like the idea of a school savings plan – that is, the pupils were encouraged to put some of their pocket money into the bank rather than spend it all. An employee from the Commonwealth Bank came around regularly; the kids all had bank deposit books; their savings were collected and entered; and they could watch their money grow, probably by something like ten or twenty cents at a time.

And then there were school fetes. Another novelty. It was all so very different from our own schooldays. And classrooms looked different, too: colourful and airy, and a bit chaotic even. In many instances the pupils didn't even sit at proper desks that were all lined up in rows, but lounged on the floor writing or drawing lying down, or they sat in groups talking, or discussing a project. Oh, gone were the days of orderly and silent classrooms when only the teacher talked and everyone listened attentively and only one pupil responded when asked!

Our boys always walked to school and back, as did nearly all children. Rarely did parents drop their children off or pick them up after school – perhaps if they had to attend some after-school activity (of which there wasn't much on offer) or if the weather was really bad. Tim tells of one such experience when he was in first or second grade: a terrific thunderstorm occurred just before school was out. Thunder and lightning had moved away when the bell went, but the rain was pelting down. Mrs S would only let those children go home who had a parent waiting outside. Tim said he did (but he didn't), and stomped home through pouring rain and every puddle on the way. He thought it was the most exciting and adventurous thing he had ever done in his young life.

We always spoke German at home; that was the language with which we were at ease with each other, and it was only natural that we spoke it with our kids as well. Tim's first language was German, although he picked up English very quickly once he went to Margaret's on the days I was working. Until he went to school, he was comfortably bilingual. But not surprisingly, with his little brother he would more often speak English than German.

As soon as Ralph was old enough to go out and play with the other children in the neighbourhood – and there were plenty of them at the time – we never heard another German word out of him. What could we do? He knew his parents spoke English and everyone else around him did, so why bother with another language? We didn't want to force the issue. So our family became bilingual in its own peculiar way. The boys spoke English to us and we spoke German to them. That went on for many years until they were virtually adults. Since then, English has become our family's language, except when Chris and I are on our own, and even then the odd English word or expression, or a miserable translation of it, creeps in. Or when – for the life of us – we cannot think of the proper German word. Tim has retained much of his knowledge of German, whereas Ralph's does not go much beyond *ja* and *nein*.

*A Canberra friend visits my parents, 1966.*

*Our house in snow, winter 1966.*

*Four generations, June 1968.*

*The four of us, summer 1968/69.*

*Gathering firewood in the Brindabellas, winter 1970.*

*Fishing in the Goodradigbee River, summer 1970/71.*

*My mother at Yarrangobilly Pool, spring 1972.*

*Lego tower, c. 1973.*

*Camping at Lake Eucumbene, c. 1974.*

*Tim and the girl next door on UN Day at school, c. 1974.*

*Getting ready to billycart down Mt Taylor, c. 1975.*

*Tim at Gibraltar Falls, c. 1975.*

*Ralph helps to cook, c. 1975.*

*Ralph's first day at school, February 1975.*

*Fetching a trolley at a German railway station, July 1975.*

*The boys at their grandparents' farm, July 1975.*

# 8

# Everyday life – lamingtons and lingerie

As in most families, everyday life for us, too, revolved around school and work, weekdays, weekends and holidays. By 1974, I was working part-time from home, so I was there when the boys returned from school, and dinner was usually on the table when Chris came home from work. Some other mothers in the neighbourhood also found part-time work. The numbers at coffee mornings or afternoons shrank. But there were compensations: we had Tupperware parties every now and then, also the occasional lingerie party or a jewellery party. I even remember a flower party – with dried flowers and related decorative items. They were usually good fun, although there was always some gentle pressure to buy so that the hostess would be entitled to an appropriate gift. There was a limit, though, to how much Tupperware a household required.

Part-time work allowed me to pursue outside interests. The variety of courses on offer had been increasing from year to year, and so I was able to refresh my knowledge of Spanish (most of which has long since been forgotten); I dabbled in painting and pottery, in decoupage and macramé, two crafts that have been all but forgotten; I did a course in photography at the then TAFE, even one called Entertaining with Elegance. I learned relaxation and yoga, and in later years attended various short writing courses and workshops. This list is by no means comprehensive, but it gives an idea of the possibilities that existed in Canberra for self-enrichment and self-development.

In the late 1970s, with a group of friends, we started to go on monthly bushwalks. This group continued for almost twenty years. Through it, as well as through membership of a formal bushwalking club, we came to know nature, its beauty and its diversity, much more closely than on any of our early Sunday drives into the countryside. And we made many new friends in the process.

Somewhere along the way, our family acquired a big blue family tent, one with two separate sleeping spaces and a living/cooking area. Now, during the long summer school holidays we spent at least two weeks at Broulee, usually the first two weeks in January. We did that for quite a number of years. The caravan park, our caravan park, no longer exists. It made room for apartments many years ago. It was a wild sort of place with barely a flat patch and none of the sites properly laid out. Amenities were basic, too, yet no one really seemed to mind. In the afternoons, the proprietor fired up the boiler so that there would be enough hot water when everyone returned from the beach. There were only two showers for the ladies, and we all queued patiently for our turn. Many families came back every year, and the kids made friends and were looking forward to seeing them again from one year to the next. Caravan parks with swimming pools, playground equipment and clipped lawns were a rarity in those days.

Broulee has, since those days, remained a firm favourite with our family. We still remember Broulee Island as a real island, out of reach unless one owned a boat. Over the years, the channel that separated the island from the mainland grew narrower and narrower, and one summer the boys used air mattresses to paddle across the few remaining metres of deep water. The following summer the channel was gone, the island no longer an island. Now, with the land bridge widening every year, a visit to Broulee always includes a walk around the island.

We also had a smaller family tent just big enough for four air mattresses and easily packed into the boot of the car. Our VW kombi had by then been traded in for a station wagon with a boot large enough to take our camping gear. While the big tent was only for long holidays at the beach, with the little one we travelled to all sorts of places near and far. It was a simple life out in nature, in the bush, and an enjoyable one. Once we camped on the shores of Lake Eucumbene at Easter. When we peeked out of the tent in the morning, the countryside around us was white with frost. Inside the small tent, with four bodies close together, we had been warm and cosy.

It took us quite a while to decide to acquire a television set. There were only a couple of channels, and most programs did not sound all that exciting. After all, we had our radio, we had records, and we had books. Why bother about a television? But once the boys started watching television next door, we felt it was time to get our own so that we could have some say in what they were watching. This would have been the very early 1970s. The boys' favourite programs were *Sesame Street* and *Humphrey B. Bear*, or at least that was what they were allowed to watch. Apart from the news, Chris and I found a few programs we liked to watch for a bit of entertainment. I remember *Dave Allen at Large* and *The Good Life*, and sometimes the boys watched with us. Until they were old enough to read their own books, we always read them a goodnight story. After that, and by a certain time, probably eight o'clock, it was definitely lights out. No exceptions.

One of their favourite and longest lasting toys were Lego blocks. In those days you couldn't buy Lego service stations or airplanes or ready-built houses that could only be demolished and then put together again in the same way. There were just simple Lego blocks – fours, sixes, twelves and so on – in various colours and a couple of sizes. The kids could let their imagination run wild in what they wanted to build: anything from little villages to a metre-high tower that was, once finished and admired, demolished with great relish.

Together, and with some advice and help from their father, the boys built a billy cart, mostly using tools from their very own toolboxes. When finished, the cart was dragged all the way up to the top of Mt Taylor in order to test its brakes on the way down. A rather heart-stopping experience for the parents who were there to watch the whole show, always at the ready should something not work to expectations. But the brakes actually worked! The boys also built a small skateboard ramp and tried it out on the footpath in front of our house. Some bruises and grazes resulted from that experiment.

Like all the children in the neighbourhood, our boys had their bikes, sometimes, but not always, handed down from older brother to younger brother. The boys would have enjoyed having a dog, but we were not keen on such a commitment. A cat lived with us for a number of years until it disappeared one day. Tim tended to a couple of goldfish for a few years, but as they kept dying – and were then ceremoniously buried in our garden – he eventually lost interest. A blue-tongue lizard turned up in our backyard during many summers relishing the snails that we collected for it.

As far as extracurricular activities were concerned, there was not terribly much on offer. After school the kids went out to play – to muck around, as they'd say – in their own backyard, at a friend's house or backyard, or down at the creek and beyond. There were no computers, either in schools or at home, no mobiles, and television was often rationed, at least in some families. There were plenty of opportunities to play and plenty of kids to play with: a whole gang in our neighbourhood, with Ralph being the youngest.

One day, a game of hide-and-seek was going on. Breathlessly, two of the girls came to our house looking for Ralph; he'd gone hiding and couldn't be found. They had looked everywhere. We looked everywhere, too, and finally found him in the wardrobe in his room where he had hidden and fallen asleep. Another time – and this was before he was at preschool – he was more than halfway up our birch tree, his latest hiding place. We tried very hard to stay calm and coax him down!

Saturdays were a different matter; no mucking around with the neighbourhood kids then. Everyone was at sports. Australians were mad about sport, I had found out. I only knew they were good at tennis, but hadn't realised until I came here that they played rather strange games like cricket and football, which wasn't what we in Germany called *Fussball* – which was soccer and not much played in those early years. Saturday was sports day for most kids – for ours, it was the day for German language school. The boys went there only reluctantly and after a few years simply refused to go. They joined Little Athletics for a while, but did not really like it all that much. We never sent them to any of the real Australian types of sports: the various codes of football or, heaven forbid, cricket. They learned to swim early, more by default than by design, and later joined a swimming club. For some years, Ralph – and to a certain degree Tim, too – was in serious training at what later became the Oasis Swimming Pool, which unfortunately closed down a few years ago. Training was for an hour early in the morning before school, and again after school, five days a week and on Saturday mornings. Then there was club night, originally with the Capital and later the Telopea Amateur Swimming Club. And there were swimming carnivals, locally as well as regionally in places like Narooma, Eden and Griffith.

Sporting and similar clubs, like schools, need money to operate. Membership fees don't go a long way. Here too, like at school, fundraising was the way to go. So, through the swimming club and the Scouts, to which Ralph belonged for a while, we became involved in this activity. One of the popular means to do that was a lamington drive. The parents would spend an evening or a weekend afternoon at a hall and roll sponge-cake squares first in melted chocolate and then in desiccated coconut. Six lamingtons to a carton (or was it ten?), wrapped in a plastic bag then distributed according to orders (or did we go from door to door and flog them?). Raffles were another means of raising dollars, and they exist to this day. Later, kids came to our door seeking sponsors for a spellathon or a walkathon to raise funds for a special school project. These did not involve any work on the part of the parents, as long as they and their friends and neighbours were generous with their donations.

As much as we took an interest in and involvement with our boys' activities, we also expected them to be part of other, family- and home-oriented activities. I think the kids used to call it work. Together we would collect pebbles at the river for the enhancement of our driveway, or mossy rocks in the bush for the garden, or we would drive into the

Brindabellas and collect firewood. Once at home, the boys would stack the wood after their father had chopped it. When we extended the house at the back, I took a photo of Tim placing roof tiles, one by one, on to the conveyor belt to be transported to their destination on top of the extension. He was nine years old at the time. Rest assured, he was not forced to do that work. The boys often wanted to be involved and useful when something that concerned their home or their family was going on. But this willingness certainly never extended to keeping their own rooms neat and tidy. That, however, is another story and one that most parents are familiar with.

In February 1968 I experienced my first really hot Australian summer. We had no air conditioning then, neither in the house nor in the car. The temperature rose to just short of forty degrees and there was not much relief to be found anywhere. Occasionally, we went to Pine Island, where the Murrumbidgee flowed deep and clear, and we spent as much time as possible in the water. If time was short, a cool-down in Lake Burley Griffin was fun, too. No blue-green algae then.

Three years later, January 1971 was a hot and humid month. Clouds built up in the afternoons and eventually a thunderstorm erupted, followed by some horrendous downpours. On several occasions, water just streamed down our driveway into the garage, which, luckily, had a side door at the far end. We stood there, barefoot, brooms in hand, sweeping the water out the side door as it flowed in. No damage done, though. But not every household was that lucky. Many houses, particularly those on hillsides, had water rushing through them, damaging floor coverings and furniture. Some afternoons I would sit with the boys in the lounge room and through the big window we would watch the lightning and hold on tight to each other when the thunder roared.

On Australia Day that year, the downpour was particularly heavy and prolonged. It was dark when the rain finally ceased. The boys had been put to bed and were sound asleep. Chris and I went outside. The air tasted wet and fresh. There was no wind, not a breath of wind, but there was another sound: the rippling of water. We followed the sound down the laneway to Peacock Place and then to Yarralumla Creek before it flowed under the McCulloch Street bridge. The concrete-lined creek, bereft of its natural course, had turned into a fast-flowing waterway, a raging torrent. Not only had it broken its banks, but it had spread way beyond them. A vast lake lay before us. There was an eerie and scary silence, broken only by the gurgling sound of flowing water. In the dark, in the distance near the bridge, we could see people moving about. We wondered what they were doing, but didn't investigate any further.

The next morning we read in *The Canberra Times* that seven young people who had tried to drive through the then low-level crossing along Yarra Glen were swept off the concrete causeway. Some had drowned in their cars; others had been swept away by the waters when they tried to get out of their vehicles. One young person was eventually found near where the creek entered the Molonglo River, downstream from Scrivener Dam. The night before, the people near the McCulloch Street bridge had formed a human chain in a vain search for survivors. Nearly four decades later, a memorial to those seven young people was erected near where they came to grief on Australia Day 1971.

As far as going out was concerned, Chris and I would occasionally go to the theatre or a concert. Not only had offerings increased dramatically since we saw *La Traviata* at the Albert Hall in 1963, so had the quality and variety since the opening of the Canberra Theatre Centre. Other venues opened as the city's population grew. Restaurants, too, kept growing in number and variety. Gus' Restaurant at the Canberra Playhouse had an unmistakably European flair. Yes, this is the same Gus who later, from his café in Garema Place, pioneered outdoor eating in Canberra by doggedly resisting all bureaucratic efforts to keep his tables and chairs off the footpath. But our restaurant visits were few and far between. As a family we were more likely to have picnics with friends or invite them for dinner – or they invited us.

The first time we had been invited to a meal in an Australian home, at Ian and Roma's way back in 1963, dinner had been in the traditional English style: meat, potatoes and two vegetables. That was not unfamiliar to us, although I think in Germany we would have had more potatoes and only one vegetable. Our food, however, would have had salt and pepper added during the cooking. Here, and not only on this first occasion, food seemed to be cooked without any spices. Salt and pepper sat on the table and were used liberally according to each person's liking. Judging by our neighbour's dining table, where the tomato sauce bottle appeared to be a permanent fixture, we decided that Australians must like tomato sauce very much, too.

Another novelty when being invited to a meal at an Australian home was the fact that the hostess served the meal on individual plates with an equal share for everyone. There were no bowls of food on the table, there were rarely second helpings and if the serving was too big, you left it on the plate, which seemed a waste to me. From a very young age we had learned that food was never to be wasted, never – just ask our kids. At home – I mean, in Germany – the food always appeared on the table in bowls or on platters and everyone helped themselves, with Mother usually serving the children. We knew quite well that whatever was on the table had to be shared by all present. So greed was not allowed. Apart from that, whatever was on your plate had to be eaten, even if it meant staying back after everyone had left the table. But there were still eyes watching until the last scrap of food had been cleaned off the plate.

And yet another novelty, one that took me quite a few years to get used to, was that people offered to bring something, meaning food, when they were invited to a meal. Food, according to my German upbringing, was entirely the responsibility of the hosts. How could you ask your guests to bring some food? I have long since changed my mind on that and for certain occasions find it a wonderful idea, especially, of course, for parties with a good number of guests. It spreads the workload around and not only the guests, but the host and hostess too, can be more relaxed and enjoy the company of their guests rather than rushing around all the time, making sure that everyone has enough to eat and enough to drink. Australian parties are really quite relaxed, with guests helping themselves to food and drink. A great way to go.

That brings me to another matter: organisations would often ask attendees to bring a plate for a meeting of one kind or another. Apparently, it has actually happened that someone brought a plate, just a simple plate, expecting, I presume, that food would be available after the meeting. How were newcomers to this country – or to the English language – supposed to know that to bring a plate meant to bring a plate with something on it to share?

To go to a restaurant meal with a bottle of wine in a paper bag tucked under your arm was another new experience for us. No such concept existed in Germany, because licensing laws were different. Here BYO was, and usually still is, a great idea.

All these minor cultural differences – do they really matter? Of course not. We are all different in our own ways, and it's the differences that make getting to know each other and learning to get along with each other more challenging, more interesting and ultimately more rewarding.

# 9

# Going home – $800 and thirty-six hours one way

When I stood on the railing as the *Fairsea* moved down the river towards the open sea on that 22 May 1962, I wondered whether I would ever see those familiar shores again. Would I ever see my parents again? My family? My friends? Those flat expanses of northern Germany that had become my home after the war? The birch trees? The oaks? The meadows and the fields? I doubted it. Australia was simply too far away, the other end of the earth.

Busy first years followed my arrival. There was the wedding, my first job, our home in Curtin, my second job, the weekend explorations of our surroundings near and far, and all the excitement and challenges that went with these events. Thinking of home had somehow slipped into the background. When our first child was born, the thoughts of home on the other side of the globe surfaced again. My parents should see and get to know their first grandchild. We determined to save up so that at least two – if not all three – of us could go for a visit. I went back to work part-time as soon as I could after Tim's birth. Chris was not greatly interested in returning to Germany for another visit and indicated that he was quite happy for me and Tim to go once we had saved enough money. But save we must.

Occasionally, very occasionally, someone we knew went home for a visit. Most of these visits then were to family and perhaps friends, rarely to see the sights or a slice of the wider world. Those with enough time went by boat, as flying was still expensive. Konrad, the cabinetmaker, the man who had made all that solid furniture for us which we still have today, took his wife and five-year-old daughter to Europe by boat in 1966. They stayed away a whole year, with Konrad working in the family's carpentry business, and the family visiting friends and relatives as the occasions arose. We had given him the address of my parents as well as those of Chris's brothers, and Konrad actually took the time to visit them. It meant so much to us that someone from Canberra would visit our families and tell them about us, tell them all those everyday things that could never be satisfactorily covered or conveyed in letters. This was a personal touch that, although indirect, meant more than words on a page could ever say. Letters were then the only thread that connected us with our families over there. These visits by friends were another, although more sporadic, one. Konrad must have realised the importance of his mission, because he travelled all the way to northern Germany from his family home in the south to see my family; Chris's brother did not live far from Konrad's family.

Then news came of charter flights being organised by the German Club in Sydney, and gradually more detailed information trickled through. At $800 for a return flight this was certainly more affordable than a regular flight, but it still represented a considerable slice of our income. By now I was, of course, on more than the £18 ($36) a week I had earned at Philips, and we were, after all, a two-income family. But with a small child, a mortgage and a seemingly never-ending list of things still to be done to house and garden or still to be acquired, we had to watch our expenditure carefully and adopt a strict savings regime. I am not sure whether it was already possible then, but it certainly became fashionable a decade or so later that one would travel now and pay later, that is, take out a loan for something considered non-essential, a luxury, and repay on return. Not in our wildest dreams would we have done something as frivolous as that!

Gradually, our savings grew. Details of flights were obtained and a deposit was paid. Seeing we were paying all that money, we wouldn't just go for a few weeks. We might as well make the most of it, so the thinking went, and stay at least four months. Yes, four months. And that was particularly poignant because only Tim and I were going. Chris would stay home, mind house and garden and keep working.

It was 1968. We left in May, barely a month after Tim's first birthday, and returned around the middle of September. Of course, the flight was with Lufthansa, but what a long flight it was! Thirty-six hours from Sydney to Frankfurt with stops in Singapore, Bangkok, Bombay (now Mumbai), Karachi and Athens. It was anything but easy travelling with a one-year-old who had just learned to walk and in every waking minute wanted to practise his new skill rather than sit on his mother's lap. There were no cots, or, if there were any, we didn't score one. And there was not a single spare seat, so I had to hold Tim on my lap throughout the whole flight. I can't remember how we managed the meals! As it turned out, we were not the only mother-and-child duo. Other mothers had similar problems to mine, but somehow we all managed and eventually we arrived in Frankfurt on a bright spring morning.

It did feel as if I had come home. Everything around me was familiar: the language, the way people dressed, the shopfronts, the street signs, even the pale blue and forever hazy sky. May is a beautiful month in Germany, when there is fresh green everywhere and parks and gardens are bursting with colour, when the apple trees are flowering and the chestnuts and the fragrant linden trees. I felt enveloped by the familiar, its warmth and its voice. It felt good to be home.

During those four months in Germany, Tim and I initially stayed with my parents on the farm, where there was plenty of room for visitors and always something to do to keep us occupied. My parents with their farming land and their pigs and cows and chickens, their extensive vegetable garden, their orchard and the pub they were managing were always very busy. So I just went along with their everyday routines and pitched in where necessary. My two sisters were by then living away from home, but often returned on weekends. My eleven-year-old brother, however, was still there. He became Tim's much admired playmate. Relatives, family friends and some of my friends from schooldays came to visit, some of them bringing their own small children. When Aunt Elisabeth, my mother's sister and my godmother, came and hugged me, she said, 'I never thought I'd see you again.' Yes, Auntie, same here. During my brother's summer school holidays, my mother managed to prise herself away from work for a week and we went on a beach holiday to the Baltic Sea.

Some weeks after our arrival, my parents celebrated their silver wedding anniversary. Not only were all the relatives invited – and most of them came – but half the village as well. My maternal grandmother, aged seventy-six, was there. Tim was her first great-grandchild, and we have a lovely photo of four generations posing among the flowers.

Eventually the time came to visit Chris's family in the south of Germany: his two brothers and his mother, his father having passed away some fifteen months earlier. We travelled by train, which generally worked quite well; at least we always had enough room, as most passengers tended to give a wide berth to a mother travelling with a child or children. Difficulties only arose when we had to change trains, because handling a small child, a suitcase, a stroller and a handbag was not always easy. However, amazingly, there usually was help at hand from fellow travellers or station attendants.

Wherever we stayed with relatives, Tim became the centre of attention, there being no other small child around, only cousins in their late teens who enjoyed amusing a one-year-old when he was having a bath or pushing the stroller when we went for walks.

I had a letter from Chris almost every week and sent him one just as regularly, the telephone still being unaffordable. Somehow it was as if I was gradually sliding back into my old German ways. It felt more and more natural being where I was. Every time a letter came from Chris, however, I was reminded that where I was at the time was not my home, not any more. My home was on the other side of the globe and before long, I – no, we – would be returning there.

And return we did, on another crowded charter flight along the same route with the same five stops. Chris, who had dropped us off at Sydney airport four months earlier, was there to meet us and take us back to Canberra in our VW kombi. It was good to be back.

A few years later, our old-time friends Max and Gerda took off on their first trip to Germany. They went by air leaving from Canberra and we, together with some other friends, saw them off at the airport. We were all very excited, not just the ones leaving, but the ones staying behind too. When Max and Gerda returned a couple of months later, we were all there again to welcome them. It was a very exciting occurrence to meet or see someone off on an overseas flight, which occasionally even warranted a bit of bubbly to calm the butterflies. My sisters had the bubbly ready at Frankfurt airport when I left, but I don't think it would have been allowed here. And when friends came back and had been taken home, we sat around – now definitely with bubbly – and watched them unpack and show off the exciting things they had purchased overseas. Today, with so many people travelling the world and with airport regulations and security being so much tighter, departures and arrivals have become rather mundane occurrences; and friends are often only taken to the airport departure point or picked up in order to save on the taxi fares. No great celebrations any more.

Our first overseas trip as a family was around Christmas 1974 when we visited my friend Rosemarie, the girl I had first met in the Bremerhaven migrant hostel and with whom I had shared a cabin on the *Fairsea*. She and her family lived in Wanaka on New Zealand's South Island. Rosemarie had married an Englishman; they had two small children, slightly younger than ours. They were building a house in Wanaka and, at the time of our visit, were living in the two-room garage: one bedroom and a kitchen-cum-living area. It reminded us of our tiny bedsitter in Campbell. We had brought our small four-person A-frame tent along and pitched it inside the roof- and floorless frame of their house-to-be. This was where we slept. Luckily it rarely ever rains in Wanaka, and it never did during our stay. Even though it sounds crowded with four adults and four children in two rooms, it was good fun. The children were outside most of the time, and in the kitchen the big table had enough room for all of us to sit at.

I went to Germany again in 1975, seven years after my first visit.

This time I took both Tim and Ralph, then aged eight and six, and we stayed away for two months. Chris still did not want to come and again stayed home, minded house and garden and went to work. It was a great age to be travelling with the boys. They had their own seats, they knew about and had met at least a few of their German family who had come to visit us in Australia, and they were interested and old enough to know something about the wider world; for example, two of the things they wanted to do were to climb the Eiffel Tower and to see the big mountains of Switzerland. They were also fairly independent creatures and gradually became quite travel-savvy. We had Eurail passes and could travel virtually anywhere we liked on the continent. Very tempting.

The boys had soon worked out a method we used when boarding a train and when alighting. As soon as the train had come to a halt, both the boys would rush in as nimbly as they could and find us seats or a suitable compartment; one boy would stay to claim the space, the other return to fetch me and the luggage. When we arrived at a station, one of the boys was always among the first ones off to go in search of a luggage trolley. We never lost each other which, with hindsight, I find quite surprising considering the crowds at most European railway stations.

Yes, we went to Paris and the boys climbed, or at least went up, the Eiffel Tower. We crossed from Switzerland into Austria, and they saw the big mountains. They explored medieval castles, fed squirrels in the forest, climbed rocks and mountains, and even showed some awe when standing inside a thousand-year-old cathedral. We travelled all the way north to Copenhagen, where we admired the rather unassuming little mermaid and where Ralph experienced a big disappointment: on a city sightseeing tour we stopped to watch the changing of the guard in front of the palace. When it was all over, he blurted out his disappointment; he had expected the guards to change their clothes.

In Germany we were sometimes asked how it was possible that the boys were allowed out of school for a whole two months. There were school holidays during that time, but still, the boys would have missed at least five weeks of school. Such an arrangement was unthinkable under the German education system. Here, the teachers had no objections. And when you think of it, the boys may have missed some spelling and arithmetic, but how much had their horizons expanded, how much more did they know about the world now?

We had actually started this particular trip with a three-day stopover in Japan. On the flight from Sydney to Tokyo, the boys were asked – and this is what airlines did with interested kids and adults then – if they wanted to have a look at the cockpit. Of course, they did.

One of the most memorable moments of our brief stay in Tokyo was a meal in a typical Japanese restaurant where no one spoke English, and we of course had no knowledge of Japanese. We picked our dishes according to the pictures on the menu, and when the food was brought, there were only chopsticks to eat it with. The restaurant had no forks. I was familiar with chopsticks, Tim was valiantly trying to eat with them, but six-year-old Ralph worried that he might have to go hungry. So one of the waitresses sat down at our table and fed him and helped Tim as well.

Apart from criss-crossing parts of Europe, we of course spent time with relatives. The boys loved their stay with their grandparents best of all. A free and easy life on the farm was just what they needed after our travels. They tended to follow their grandfather everywhere; they learned to drive the tractor, fed the chickens and watched the cows being milked.

During this visit I had the opportunity to attend a school reunion. Many had come, even some of our old teachers, and none of us had changed to such an extent as to be unrecognisable to former classmates. But it was a sobering realisation that already one from our ranks was no longer alive.

I also had the opportunity to accompany my father on a brief visit to the East, to the former German province of Pomerania, which is now Poland, but which used to be our home until we had to leave it after the end of World War II. It was a strange sort of homecoming; everything still looked familiar thirty years on but the buildings were run-down and neglected, and everything was so much smaller than I remembered: the house itself, the place where I spent the first six years of my life, was smaller, the neighbour's house so much closer, the yard narrower, the garden not nearly as expansive as I had imagined. But then, it was the memory of a six-year-old that I carried within me.

Perhaps he was inspired by our trip to Europe, because not long after our return, Chris suddenly announced that he would like to go to Germany after all to see his family and friends again. He chose the northern summer of the following year, 1976, and planned to be away for seven weeks. He travelled on his own through Austria and Switzerland, then caught up with his family before travelling to northern Germany to visit his in-laws. The visit to his parents' home was not an altogether happy one. His father had passed away nine years earlier and he was shocked to see how severely affected by dementia his mother had become, even since my visit the year before. For him, home was no longer what he remembered, his memories somehow diminished by the experience. His mother passed away the following year, aged nearly eighty-three.

The following year, at the Oktoberfest raffle at the Harmonie German Club, for which Lufthansa had sponsored one low-season return flight from Sydney to Frankfurt, Chris was the lucky winner. As the ticket was not transferable, he had to go to Germany yet again! He did so in February 1978 and this time only went for four weeks. Everything was covered in snow when he arrived. He hadn't taken a winter coat simply because he did not own one; he had to borrow one from his brother. He also had to buy another jumper and a shawl and some gloves! He had forgotten how cold winters in Germany could be. He would never again go to Europe in winter, he decided. And he hasn't.

An interesting thing happened in our family during Chris's two absences. Apart from my two trips to Germany, we as a family had always done things together: picnics, weekend trips, holidays, camping. With Chris not there, the boys must have felt that somehow there was a hole that needed to be plugged. They stayed home much more than usual after school and on weekends they were more helpful around the house, often without even being asked. Were they perhaps trying to replace their father?

Ten days after his tenth birthday, Tim flew to Germany on his own to visit his grandparents, his aunts and uncles. He was away for ten weeks. There was no problem having time off from school; the only condition his teacher imposed was that he keep a diary, which he faithfully did. And whatever he missed during those ten weeks, in the overall scheme of things, it didn't matter at all. We all went to Sydney in the car and watched him being led away by a Qantas stewardess with a 'Young Passenger Travelling Alone' sign pinned to his shirt. He was very brave, we thought.

At the time, my two sisters were living in Frankfurt and one of them had been designated to collect Tim on arrival. She had to identify herself to airline staff before she could take the boy with her. Tim spent most of his time with my parents, whom he, of course, still remembered from earlier times. He still enjoyed everything the farm had to offer and still kept following his grandfather around like a shadow. Highlights were when he was allowed to ride a horse or drive the tractor to and from the fields. But he became also interested in my parents' other activity – the country pub – and would offer to help his grandmother there as she dispensed beer and schnapps. But mostly he just watched some of the old regulars play cards or dice. And occasionally, when grandmother wasn't looking, the men even let him join in. My aunt and uncle, city folk who regularly went on holidays, came for a brief visit and took Tim with them for a holiday on the Baltic coast, a highlight of which was a visit to the original Legoland. Later, one of my sisters came and picked Tim up to take him south so he could spend some time with the relatives on his father's side of the family. And before he knew it, the visit had come to an end. My sisters took him to the airport and handed him over to Qantas; once again the sign 'Young Passenger Travelling Alone' was pinned to his shirt. We collected him in Sydney some thirty or so hours later. The most exciting thing for him on the return flight between Singapore and Sydney was that he was allowed to visit the cockpit, and not only that, he was allowed to sit in the pilot's seat and pretend he was flying the plane. He was also allowed to sit in business class, which he thought was simply tops.

To be fair, what is good for one child is only fair for the other. So, three years later, when he was almost eleven, Ralph had to do what his big brother had done before him. He, however, did not want us to take him to Sydney airport. Canberra would do. He was quite confident that he would manage on his own in Sydney. In truth, he had visions of passing his transit time wandering around the duty-free shops and spending his money. But that was not to be. We handed him over to a Qantas staff member at Canberra airport, and off he went quite confidently with the 'Young Passenger Travelling Alone' note pinned to his jacket. In Sydney, at the domestic terminal, he remembers being allowed behind the check-in counter and helping move luggage along – or at least pretending to. Eventually, a stewardess collected him and took him to the international terminal, where he had to pass the time in a special room, together with three or four other children who were also travelling alone, until he was ready to board his flight. In Frankfurt, one of his aunts picked him up and he passed his ten-week stay in similar fashion to his brother. He had his eleventh birthday there which, I believe, was a rather adult event. Ralph didn't mind. His grandparents had bought him a pair of roller skates which he had pined for but was unable to use on the farm's uneven surfaces.

Three other things were different from his brother's trip. My parents were retiring and moving to their new home just outside the village. This move was quite an exciting event for a boy who was always keen to make himself useful. Like Tim, Ralph also visited his uncles, Chris's brothers, but as there was no one available to take him by car to one of them, he was simply put on a train, told where and at what time to get off – Ralph had a watch – and his uncle was waiting for him at the other end. There was no changing of trains involved, though. The final difference was that I travelled to Germany – and a few places in-between, the travel bug having well and truly bitten by then – some four weeks after Ralph, and we flew home together. He now considered himself a world traveller.

One of Ralph's most memorable discoveries from this trip was that he became aware of the fact that he had a big family over on the other side of the globe. There were not only grandparents and aunts and uncles, but cousins, some of whom were twice his age and others only half his age; there were great uncles and great aunts and second-degree cousins and there were two distinct branches of the family – the paternal and the maternal side. Here in Australia, our children had grown up without relatives. Even though they had met some of them, it had always only been for short periods of time. The boys had never been fully aware that relatives are part of your place in the world, of your background and your heritage; that relatives turn up for family celebrations and you are expected to come to theirs. Sure, we had friends here, but – for better or worse – they were not the same as relatives.

Over the years, I have on occasions been asked where home actually is. And every time we visited Germany, we always talked about going home. Not any more. In the northern winter of 1992, I flew to Germany for my mother's seventy-fifth birthday. When I boarded the return flight at Frankfurt, I came to sit next to a young Australian girl who had been on a student exchange. 'I'm going home,' she said when I asked where she was going. 'So am I,' I said, and I felt my heart doing a little jolt. I suddenly realised the full implication of those three words. Yes, I was going home, home to Australia, to Canberra, to our house in Curtin, to my family. That's where I belonged. Yet it was going to be quite a few years before that status of belonging was eventually formalised.

## 10

## Visitors – a welcome on the tarmac

In the early years, we sometimes wondered whether anyone from home would ever come to visit. Would anyone want to travel that far and pay that much money to come and see us? We doubted it very much, just as we initially doubted that we would ever again visit the family back home. But our doubts were soon dispelled.

Our very first visitor was a cousin of mine, Reimer, a toolmaker by trade, who had migrated to Canada in the late 1950s and now wanted to sound out Australia and its employment opportunities. We had no spare bed for him nor, of course, any spare space in our tiny flat. But our landlady pitched in. My cousin was allowed to sleep on the floor in one of their empty rooms upstairs. He didn't mind. Reimer liked Australia, particularly the climate after coming from cold Canada; but as far as work opportunities were concerned, he found that trade union dominance in his particular field would make things difficult for him. He returned to Canada and lives there still.

Rosemarie and a friend turned up one day. The young ladies were on their way to Thredbo for a working stint in the snow season. They also slept on the floor in the landlady's spare room upstairs. They called in again once the snow season had finished and Rosemarie's contracted two years in Australia were up. She was ready to move on. New Zealand was her next destination and, after travelling much of the world, she eventually returned with a husband and a child to settle there.

Our first visitors in our Curtin home were friends of Chris's from Geelong: his former landlord and young son. They slept on the floor of our second bedroom. We didn't as yet have any spare beds, only a pair of air mattresses. That sufficed.

When the next visitors came, in the summer of 1969 – and this time they really came all the way from Germany – we did have spare beds. The visitors were classmates of mine, a husband and wife. He was employed by Lufthansa, and they were travelling on the cheap. For me, this was a visit from home, not yet by family, but from home nonetheless. We talked a great deal about family and friends in Germany, although the visitors were also curious to learn about Australia. They were as ignorant about the country as I had been when I first arrived. Somehow, through their short visit, they gave us the feeling that home was not so far away, not so unreachable after all.

A year later, my university friend Erika and her partner Bruno arrived. They were not visitors or tourists; they were migrating to Australia. They spent several weeks with us, wanting to accustom themselves to Australian conditions and the Australian way of life. Their final destination, however, was not going to be Canberra but Brisbane. They had had enough of cold and grey German winters. They wanted sunshine and warmth all year round. As an engineer, Bruno soon found employment with the Brisbane City Council, where he remained until his retirement. The two are still living in Brisbane, and we are still friends.

Our first family visitor was my sister Christiane, who arrived in July 1970 on a kind of student exchange, which wasn't really an exchange at all. She was studying graphic design at the Hanover School of Art, where she had heard about the possibility of going to Australia for three months' work experience in her chosen field, providing she had family there. I think the terms of this exchange were quite loose, as Christiane actually only worked for about a month; she spent another month travelling on her own to places we had never been to, like the Whitsundays, and the remainder of the time she was with us. For her work experience, the department – or whoever administered this particular scheme – had found her a job as a window decorator at the Woolworths variety store in Civic, a shop that has long since disappeared.

Christiane's arrival in Canberra turned out to be quite an event.

When we arrived at Canberra airport to meet her, we found that the press was there to report on the arrival of a German exchange student. We were allowed to wander out on to the tarmac to meet my sister. With one-year-old Ralph in my arms and Chris holding Tim's hand, we arrived at the plane's stairs just as she appeared at the door. And the press was right there too. We were all so terribly excited to see each other again that we ignored everything else around us, except the photographer who kept insisting that my sister kiss the baby so he would have an action photo for next day's paper.

Another memorable event of my sister's visit was the weekend she agreed to mind the boys so that Chris and I could have a few days off. We went to Ulladulla. It was late winter, the motels were quiet, the beaches deserted. And I didn't want to do much more than sleep. I went back to bed after breakfast as well as after lunch, and we had an early night to boot. In my remaining waking hours we went for walks on the beach and had some lovely meals. I never realised how tiring it could be to keep house and work part-time while raising two lively boys.

Christiane has been back to Australia many times: in 1980 with her husband and six-month-old daughter Maja; nine years later she came with her husband and three children, which was a very lively, if not to say chaotic, visit; in 1999 she came with her youngest daughter, Dunja, travelling to the Red Centre during their stay; and in 2009 she came by herself visiting her sisters and her nieces and nephews around the country from Perth to Canberra to Sydney to Newcastle and Brisbane, repeating a similar trip three years later.

You see, I have another sister, Sigrun, who first came to visit us in 1977, and – because she liked it here – she came again, this time with her two-year-old daughter Geraldine, in 1982. Two years later she emigrated to Australia and lived in Canberra for twenty years before moving to Brisbane in 2004.

My mother, who liked to go places and didn't seem to mind long hours in planes, came in 1972 for the first time. In the 1980s she visited us twice, with one visit overlapping that of my father by two weeks. At home, in Germany, on the farm, even in retirement, there were daily chores, and the work was never-ending. This was the reason why my parents never came together, with this one exception, and why they never stayed more than four weeks. The two-week overlap was only possible because my mother's sister and her husband had volunteered to look after the house, the garden and the animals – chickens, geese and sheep – during their absence. It did work out, but not quite without drama: sheep escaped and a storm brought down trees in the night, luckily with only minor damage. But my city-living aunt and uncle were quite stressed out about it all and decided that country life really wasn't for them. They never offered to mind the farm again.

On her first visit to Australia, when she was fifty-four, all my mother wanted to do was to be at the beach, so she could return home with a suntan; and she wanted to frolic in the waves as much as possible. So, apart from showing her around the sights of Canberra and surroundings, including a visit to the mountains, we spent a week at various spots along the South Coast with her. When we warned her about sun exposure, she wouldn't listen, not until she was as red as a crab and began to shiver. When she was here some years later together with my father for two short weeks, I flew to Noosa with them. This time my mother was more careful about exposing herself to the sun, but it was hard to keep her away from the water. Reluctantly, she agreed to use sun cream. 'We never use that stuff at home,' she said. My father, who was not a beach person, still found enough to interest him at Noosa; most of all he loved the outdoor spa at the resort where we were staying. He said his old and tired bones really appreciated the warm water, and he was always reluctant to come out.

On my mother's third visit, it was once again the beach. My sister Sigrun was still living in Canberra then, and my mother was shared between her two daughters. My mother's last visit was in 1995 when she was seventy-seven years old. She came with her oldest granddaughter Maja, because she no longer felt confident enough to travel on her own, but she still wanted to come to Australia one more time. This time we took her to Lord Howe Island where, apart from the beach, she enjoyed the colourful fish on our glass-bottom boat trips.

This visit nearly ended in disaster. Because of the demands of school, Maja had to return to Germany earlier than originally planned. No extra holidays were allowed. My mother wanted to stay on. Flying home would be simple, she thought. We would put her on the right plane in Sydney and all she had to do was change planes at Heathrow (she was flying British Airways) to get back to Hanover in Germany. Easy. My mother announced that, according to her itinerary, she had to be at Sydney airport at three p.m.; the plane was due to leave at five p.m. We had a leisurely drive down the Hume Highway, stopping for a picnic lunch on the way. It was ten minutes to three when Chris parked the car near the British Airways departures entry. My mother and I climbed out, took the luggage and walked into the departure hall while Chris parked the car.

The departure hall was deserted. My heart sank. What was happening? In the far corner we spotted two women behind a counter. I ran across and breathlessly asked for my mother's flight. 'We've called her name many times without response,' the attendant said. 'I think it's too late. The doors have probably closed. The plane is due to depart at three p.m.' My mother caught up with me while the attendant was on the phone. A stewardess suddenly came running, grabbed my mother's suitcase. The attendant grabbed my mother's arm. 'We'd better run,' she said. And they were gone. There was no chance to say goodbye. Apparently, the cabin door had not yet been completely closed.

My mother later said she cried for hours afterwards, and when she arrived in London, she wandered aimlessly through the terminal not knowing where her flight to Germany would depart from. 'Everyone spoke English,' she said. 'I didn't know what to do.' So she sat down and cried a bit more. Eventually a young man asked her if she needed help. He took her to the right departure lounge and she eventually arrived home, but no, she was never going to come to Australia again.

My father's first visit occurred in the summer of 1979, when he was sixty-seven years old. He was a rather reluctant traveller, but he did want to see how we were doing down under. He found the cheapest possible flight with a Yugoslav airline that involved a six-hour stopover in Belgrade in each direction. However, he took it all in his stride. On this first visit, we introduced him to our world: our friends, our city, the markets, and a bit of the coast and the mountains. He confided that after the war, having lost his home and his farm in the East, he had often thought of leaving Germany and settling somewhere else, starting a totally new life in Australia or in South America; it didn't really matter as long as it was a long way away from the devastation of his country. But my mother had never been open to that idea.

On his second visit in 1984, after the week in Noosa with my mother, what my father really wanted to see in Australia were farms and farming practices. So, among many other places, we took him to Victoria, where he could inspect irrigation practices, something not needed in rain-rich northern Germany. We sometimes wondered how he would have coped had he come to Australia after the war and started farming here. It would have all been so different: the climate, the soil, the crops, the weeds, the general farming practices. Apart from the language, he would have had to learn many new things.

My father came again in 1991, departing Germany the day after his eightieth birthday. No cheap airline this time and the quickest possible flight (Qantas) to Darwin, where our eldest son then lived and where I flew to meet him. Without a hitch he managed to change planes in Bangkok and arrived in Darwin in his winter woollens – it was November. Darwin and surrounds were alien to him, though. The hot and humid climate bothered him, and he found the sudden sunsets and the sudden darkness rather disconcerting. He preferred the long dusks and dawns at home. The Red Centre where we went next was also alien to him, but held more interest. When we stood in front of Ayers Rock (Uluru), he wondered whether he was expected to climb up there. I assured him he wasn't. We continued to Adelaide because he particularly wanted to see Hahndorf and its German heritage. He dismissed it outright. 'Just a tourist village,' he said. 'Nothing particularly German about it, apart perhaps from the cuckoo clocks for sale.'

When my father was here on his first visit and we were swimming pool regulars because the boys were in training, I tried to encourage him to come along and maybe even learn to swim. He came, he was sixty-seven then, and tried; but no good. Even though he had grown up in a coastal village, his family never went to the beach; all he had known all his life was work.

We also introduced my father to take-aways and specifically to fish and chips, which were then still served wrapped in newspaper. He thought this a rather barbaric custom. Even picnics did not really appeal to him; in his world a meal was to be taken indoors where there were no flies, at the table, on plates, with proper cutlery.

On his last visit, my father brought with him a handful of acorns from a tree on his farm. He wanted to plant German acorns in Australian soil; preferably in our garden. This would always remind me of where I had come from, he said. It would be a kind of connection between there and here. We did plant a few acorns, but nothing happened; a fully grown oak tree on our block would have been impossible.

There were, of course, also visits from Chris's side of the family. The first one was a real surprise: in February 1982 his oldest brother, Rudi, rang to inform us that he intended to come to Chris's fiftieth birthday in April and that he would want to kill a pig and make sausages. Real German-style sausages, even though he was not a butcher but a carpenter. Nor was Rudi a traveller. He was one of those people who preferred to stay at home and, if after a lot of nagging from his wife, he finally consented to go away, they would go to an island in the North Sea, and they would go there – and nowhere else – every year for twenty years. So the fact that Rudi suddenly wanted to come to Australia left us in a state of semi-shock.

Rudi arrived in due course. Chris bought half a pig and the two men set about making sausages, crackling, lard and roasts. They were having a great time. And the friends, mostly Germans, but not exclusively, who came to the party enjoyed the hearty country-style food. Being a carpenter, Rudi was also interested to see how they did things here. When he observed the lightweight construction of brick-veneer homes, he called them matchbox houses and predicted that they wouldn't last a lifetime.

Rudi, in fact, enjoyed his visit so much that he promised to come again and bring his wife. And he did. They came in 1988 and again two years later. They wanted to see Sydney as well as spend some time at the beach. Despite their island holidays, they never went for a swim in the surf because of the North Sea's cold water. It took quite a bit of coaxing to get them into the water at Kioloa, but in the end they agreed that the South Pacific certainly was not the North Sea. During their 1990 visit, the four of us flew to Cairns so they could see a different part of Australia. Leni, Rudi's wife, was an avid nature lover and was thrilled by the flora of north Queensland, by the many colourful butterflies and the masses of bright and busy birds.

On their last visit together, in the autumn of 1994, Leni was suffering from abdominal cancer but had her doctor's permission to travel one more time. For their six-week stay, she had three wishes: a concert at the Sydney Opera House, a harbour cruise and a visit to the Blue Mountains. All three were achieved, with the concert providing the only, but luckily not insurmountable, obstacle. When I phoned the Opera House (this was pre-Internet), all they had available for the particular weekend's concert were two tickets with seating behind the orchestra. On the day, I managed to obtain for Chris and me two out of twenty standing-room tickets. We stood for perhaps the first ten minutes of the concert, then discovered several empty seats which nobody had come to claim. Rudi and Leni enjoyed the concert enormously, as well as the harbour cruise the next day and the vistas and views of the Blue Mountains. The weather had been kind to us every single day.

Leni passed away in August 1994, only four months after their return from Australia. Rudi came to Australia one more time, this time travelling with his ex-son-in-law, and under Chris's guidance the three men set off on a trip to Tasmania.

Other relatives and friends have come to visit us over the years, but none have ever been as exciting for us as the earliest visitors. My brother, eighteen years my junior, has been here four times, usually only popping in for short periods because he is always coming from somewhere else or going somewhere else. However, he has managed to be here for both our sons' weddings; in 2004 in Daylesford and in 2010 in Perth.

My friend from primary school days, Renate, came in 1997. It was her first overseas visit and her only one. My nieces, Christiane's daughters, came for the wedding in Perth. Our Finnish friend, the one who did her nursing training at Royal Canberra Hospital and who returned to Finland in the early 1970s, came twice to see how life had shaped up for us down under and how the children had grown in whom she had always taken a special interest. Then there have been friends of friends calling in so say hello, or grand nieces on a working holiday in Australia, or distant cousins taking a day off from their guided tour of Australia to have lunch with us, or other cousins passing through Canberra on their way along the east coast of Australia in their hire car.

And others are still to come; or so they say. Every time we go to Germany, someone will express their intention, wish or dream to come to Australia. Some of them eventually will; but others will just continue dreaming.

# 11

## The years fly past – a citizen at last

And so the years went by. The 1980s passed, the 1990s came, and a new century began; a new century that had seemed a lifetime away when we were young. And now here it was. Time simply seemed to have flown.

Our boys finished primary school, went on to high school and then to college. They obtained their professional or trade qualifications: Tim as a photographer and Ralph as a boilermaker. They moved out of home and spread their wings in Australia and the wider world. Ultimately they found their place, their very own niche. Interestingly, they both work in occupations that are distinctly Australian: Tim is involved with the world of Aboriginal art and Aboriginal art centres, mostly in Western Australia, and Ralph with big machines in the resources sector in the same state. Tim married Carly, a Tasmanian, in August 2004 in Daylesford. There was no church wedding. It was never an issue for him, despite his concerns as a primary school pupil. His younger brother married Julie, originally from the UK, in Perth in March 2010, also at a civil ceremony. And since May 2011 we are the proud grandparents of Evie Mae, Ralph and Julie's first child.

After my mother's visit in 1972, I gave office work away for a while. I worked from home, providing materials and services to Canberra's hobby potters. Pottery was a very popular hobby in the 1970s. Beginners' classes sprang up everywhere. I took part in one myself and found that most organisations offering such classes had no kilns for firing the works of their students. Here was an opportunity. We bought a kiln (and later a second one) and offered firing services. And once potters needed glazes or started to experiment with making their own, they found that the required materials were not available anywhere in Canberra. They had to be ordered from Sydney or perhaps even Melbourne. So here I came in once again. I would order clay, ready-made glazes, even some pottery tools, from a wholesaler in Sydney and display them in our converted garage. I would also order a variety of raw materials in bulk from the same wholesaler and then divide the big bags into smaller quantities, say fifty grams of iron oxide or five kilograms of dolomite. I was also the agent for a brand of kiln as well as for a pottery wheel. Pottery wheels could also be hired from me.

It was an interesting time. I learned much about the craft and met many fascinating people along the way. Hobby courses continued to flourish, pottery was taught in many schools, and the Canberra School of Art had introduced accredited ceramics courses. Some of the teachers, as well as prospective ceramicists, became my customers. I was home all day, but certainly not isolated. When the boys returned from school, I was there, and I could do the work in house and garden during the week, so that the whole family could enjoy weekends unencumbered by shopping, cleaning and gardening. I never made much money, but that didn't really matter.

By the end of the decade, I'd had enough of handling dusty raw materials, sticky clay and people's fragile works of art. It was time to go back to office work. I soon found a part-time position with a small consulting firm in Civic, consisting of only two men. For me it was a tough start: at my last office job nearly ten years earlier, electric typewriters had just started to appear on our desks. Now there were computers, and I had never seen one before. The interviewer had asked me if I could type, which I could. But he had not asked me if I could use a computer. I was terrified. One of the two men, Graeme, did his best to induct me into the mysteries of this newest piece of office equipment. What made his explanations particularly difficult for me to understand was that he had written the computer programs himself; there was no user manual, and he spoke in a jargon using words I had never heard before. What was a cursor? What did saving mean? After a few days of floundering, I felt that I was not suitable for the job; I had missed the boat as far as modern technology was concerned, and I told the men so. They encouraged me to persevere, just like Mr W of Philips had done many years ago. 'We'll talk again in a few weeks,' they said.

And one day, perhaps a week or so after our talk, it just clicked. It was like a revelation, a discovery. I see – that's how it works. It was easy after that. The firm expanded rapidly over the next year or so and opened branch offices in Sydney and Melbourne. They continued to use their home-made word processing software in all three offices, and I compiled a user manual for the benefit of my counterparts in the two branches.

The Canberra office was also expanding, and the initial dark and claustrophobic office space in Civic – because of a lack of outside windows – was no longer big enough. A move had been planned for a while. This was only my third job in Australia, but now my fourth move with my employer was imminent. With Philips I had moved from Civic to Kingston, with ICEM from Barton to Red Hill to Civic, and now I would be moving from Civic to Woden. We moved to very spacious and airy office accommodation in Corinna Chambers, where we were the only non-medical business in the whole building. I could have cycled to work if I'd had a bicycle; I could even have walked the four kilometres, but I drove to work, because parking was provided in the building's basement.

I stayed with the firm for seven years. When I left, the good times seemed to be on the wane; consulting contracts became harder to obtain; some staff members left; others began to work from home; the branch offices shrank, as did the Canberra office. Finances were tight. I knew, because I was keeping the books.

Chris and I took time out and went on an extended overseas trip. We had been married for twenty-five years and decided to go 'home' to celebrate this anniversary with family and friends, the ones I had missed so much on our wedding day.

On our return I found employment at a research centre at the Australian National University. I stayed with them for a full ten years, never moving to another location, and finally earning my three months' long-service leave. A few days after my sixtieth birthday I went to work for the very last time.

Chris, meanwhile, had left Wormalds in the early 1970s and joined the Australian National University as a fire alarm technician, later to become its fire and safety officer. He continued to be on call here, too, but, because of an extra staff member, only every third week was a stay-at-home week for him. He took early retirement at the end of 1988. After a suitable break he found other employment and eventually retired ten years later.

Shortly after Chris had joined Wormalds in 1966, it was discovered that he would not be allowed to access the Russell Hill complex in order to service the fire alarm systems because he was not an Australian citizen. Due to the urgency of the matter, he was naturalised only a week or so later in a private ceremony in an Immigration Department official's office. There was no citizenship test then, possibly not even an application fee needed to be paid, just the oath of allegiance and a handshake.

Under normal circumstances, somewhere down the track, we would have decided that the time had come for us to become Australian citizens, and we would have applied together and attended the ceremony together. As it was, I became the foreigner in our family. Not that it ever presented any problems or difficulties with work. I had permanent residency in this country, but I could not vote – which may or may not have been an advantage. When we travelled overseas, wherever we arrived and had to go through Immigration, we always stayed together in the same queue, whichever was the shorter one – the one for European passport holders or the one for those holding other passports.

But the time eventually came for me to take a stand, to decide where I really belonged. So towards the end of 2008 I put in my application to become an Australian citizen. Because of my age, I didn't have to take the test, and the fee was also waived. The ceremony took place on 7 February 2009 in Garema Place in Civic as part of the Multicultural Festival. John Hargraves MLA conducted the ceremony. For me, it lacked a sense of solemnity. The decision to change nationality is rarely taken lightly, and to swear allegiance to another country, irrespective of how much you like it there, is a serious matter. The surroundings didn't help either: the festival was a noisy and crowded affair. It was also a very hot day, the day Victoria was burning. But what made the event special for me was that so many of our friends were there to share it with me. They must have realised what this day meant for me. Together with the naturalisation certificate, every new citizen was given a small gum tree to mark the occasion. Mine was a snow gum. There was no way a snow gum would have fitted into our garden, just as there had not been room for an oak tree. The snow gum is now growing healthily on a friend's property. When we checked our paperwork, we discovered that Chris's private naturalisation ceremony had taken place exactly forty-three years earlier, on 7 February 1966.

Our retirement years, which started in 1999, have been good years so far. Some time after the boys moved out, we acquired a camper-trailer and have explored many places around the country in it. We have travelled to the Red Centre and to the Gulf, we have crossed the deserts in various directions, we have skirted the coast in the east, the south and the west. We have seen another Australia out there: the open-cut mines over on the other side, the remote communities, the lonely homesteads, the dry riverbeds and the red sand dunes. This vast and seemingly empty land upon which we looked as something intimidating, uninviting, even forbidding, has, with each trip, become more familiar. We have grown fonder of it and come to feel more at home in it.

We also continue to enjoy exploring the wider world and, as we both still have family in Germany, we have been going there fairly regularly since retirement.

We still live in the same house. But it has undergone many a metamorphosis over the decades. We have added rooms, one at the back, one at the front; we have shifted and shortened the ceiling-high doors, knocked down walls and changed windows. We wallpapered every room, then, some years later peeled the wallpaper off again and applied coats of paint. We went with the trendy colours of the times, mission brown and orange being very popular for a while; then it was back to pastels and even white, almost the same look the house originally had. The trusty Rayburn wood heater made way for something more modern – and less efficient. We installed a new kitchen and updated the old bathroom. We now have a proper bathtub that you can stretch out in for a good soaking. We have added a large deck, where we can entertain friends or have a quiet breakfast in the morning sunshine. Consequently, the back garden has shrunk in size, but that's okay.

Compared to today's large homes, or rather mansions, however, ours is still a very modest house, but it is more than ample for the two of us, and there is space for visitors too.

In all those years we've lived here, we have been burgled twice, with another attempted burglary. These all happened in the 1980s when the suburb was full of teenagers. Whether it was someone who knew our family and knew our house is hard to say. But the burglar knew what he was looking for. He (or she?) may have just overheard one of our boys mentioning to a friend that his parents had a jar full of old fifty-cent pieces, the round ones with the high silver content, standing on a kitchen shelf. In any case, the jar was gone plus a few other things, notably some of my jewellery and a bottle of whisky, but at least the burglar or burglars did not trash the place.

Our front lawn which many years ago we worked so hard to make perfectly weed-free has disappeared altogether because of water restrictions and too many weeds. None of our three birch trees has survived the drought. We again grow a few herbs and vegetables in the back garden, and when we find mushrooms near the creek, we pick them; when we see fruit trees with their branches bent low and heavy with fruit which no one is picking, we feel tempted to knock on the owner's door to ask if we would be allowed to pick the fruit, but so far we have not been brave enough.

We have never regretted that we chose to stay in Canberra rather than move to Adelaide. We have seen the city grow, expand and stretch in all directions. Sometimes we wish it would stop growing, yet with its lake shores and nature parks, it still provides many places for quiet reflection. Nor is the real bush ever far away. Canberra really provides a wonderful balance between nature and culture. I wish my English host lady, the one who told me in 1961 that Australia had no culture, could be here now to see for herself. On the cultural front, we here in Canberra are now blessed with on almost overwhelming choice of exhibitions, concerts, plays and talks. And theatres have cloakrooms and tiered seating, and there is wine, sparkling or still, on offer. All very sophisticated!

Shopping is no longer what I, in the early days, used to call detective work. The choice these days – be it furniture, wedding dresses, coffee, wine, continental smallgoods – is sometimes overwhelming. There is too much of it.

Some of our old habits, habits inculcated in childhood, have persisted: we have remained frugal and abhor waste of any kind. Food is never thrown out. Once you have experienced hunger – and I don't mean the hunger when there is nothing suitable in the fridge; I mean the hunger when there is no fridge, when the pantry is empty and a piece of bread will have to do for the day – once you have experienced that sort of hunger, food forever becomes a very precious commodity.

Also, as long as we can repair something ourselves, it will be repaired, even if it is a fifty-year-old toaster. We still love our brown bread and enjoy the varieties that are available today. The same applies to the sausages and salamis. And to cakes too. We do not very often cook genuine German food any more; other spices, tastes and flavours have crept in, notably those from the Mediterranean and, particularly, from Asia. Chris took over the cooking once he retired, and I am happy to leave the kitchen and the food shopping to him. Both his older brothers relieved their wives of the cooking when they retired. It must run in the family, although their father would not have wanted to be seen near the kitchen, nor would most other German men of Chris's generation.

For many years we continued to celebrate Christmas in the traditional German way on Christmas Eve. When the boys were still in primary school, we suggested that perhaps we should switch to the Australian way and have our presents on Christmas Day. They were not in favour. They liked the idea of having their Christmas presents ahead of their friends. But now, with two daughters-in-law of Anglo-Saxon background, we do celebrate in the Australian way, or perhaps even the English way, with noisy crackers and silly hats, and with a combination of food from all three countries.

Our circle of friends has grown; there are still many German friends, but we now also count many Australians among our friends as well as some other nationalities. Some of the friends of long ago are no longer with us. Max and Hans, those guys mad about the bush and about fishing, have passed away. So has Konrad, the maker of much of our furniture. Others have moved, Gerda has remarried, and with others from either here or overseas we have lost touch for one reason or another. There have been occasions when lost friends from long ago have been rediscovered – quite an exciting experience, especially when you discover that after all those years you still share common interests.

My parents have passed away. My father, a man who loved the land with all his heart, died in 2001, only a few months short of his ninetieth birthday. My mother, lover of sun and surf and sufferer of sunburn, was ninety-three when she died in April 2011. Hard-working and thrifty people all their lives.

Telephone calls around the world are now so cheap and easy that cost is never an issue when you want to phone someone on the other side of the world, as long as one remembers the time difference.

First names in most walks of life have become the rule rather than the exception; occasionally even an official letter will address you with your first name, which I don't find quite appropriate. I also still feel some resistance when a twenty-one-year-old in whatever official capacity addresses me with my first name. Privately that would be no problem, but officially? Perhaps this is carrying familiarity too far?

And swear words? We all know what has become of them. They have become so common in the media – in film and television as well as in print, be it books or newspapers – that 'bloody' certainly raises no eyebrows, and even the 'f' word rarely does any more; it's used in movies quite liberally these days. Worse words have come on the scene. But despite all the progress we have made on many fronts, that – the swearing – is not progress, is it? On the contrary.

Someone once told me that you belong to your new country once you start dreaming in that country's language. I have been dreaming in English for many years, so I am sure I have been an Australian for much longer than my naturalisation certificate stipulates.

The world is certainly a very different place to what it was fifty years ago and so is Australia, so is Canberra. And, of course, we have changed along with it.

When we moved into our house in Curtin, most families around us were Australians. Two houses along there lived a German man with his Croatian wife, and we soon became friends. Diagonally opposite lived an Australian couple of whom it was said that they were not married – a fact worth commenting upon then. In the cul-de-sac behind us quite a number of families from England had moved in who had been brought here for various government jobs. Today, more than forty-five years later, the German man (minus his Croatian wife) and the then allegedly unmarried couple and us – we are the only original inhabitants in our neighbourhood. Some houses have changed owners several times, most former government houses have been extended and modified or knocked down (the matchbox houses that wouldn't last a lifetime, according to Chris's brother!); young families have started to move in again. Curtin is a good place to be.

# 12

# Belonging

In 2004 I was in Fremantle. I admired the welcoming walls in front of the West Australian Maritime Museum and found my name there. I stood at the pier and tried to picture the *Fairsea* as it rode at anchor in Fremantle Port more than forty years earlier. I saw myself walking down the gangway and stepping on Australian soil for the first time; and then I saw myself alone at the pier, the vessel in the distance, disappearing over the horizon, and I all alone at the edge of the continent. That was a long, long time ago.

When I left Germany for Australia in May 1962, in my luggage I carried a simple exercise book. It was to be my diary. On the first page I wrote in quite distinct letters – my handwriting is usually rather messy – 'The biggest adventure of my life'. Well, was it that?

First and foremost it was a risk. I was only vaguely aware of that at the time but, with the carefree optimism of youth, I threw it to the wind. I set off for the other side of the world to marry a man I had only known for some six months and hadn't seen for fourteen, whose face I could barely remember when, on board ship, I stared into the blue yonder and wondered how it was all going to work out. Fifty years on and we are still together. So it did work out. What contributed to it was the fact that, in the early years, we really had no one else but each other to rely upon – no family and only recent, new friends – just each other and that, I think, created a bond that has withstood the test of time.

What about the adventure side of things? It has been an adventure not only on a personal but on a more general level also. Where else in the world can you experience nature at such close quarters? Experience the wide open spaces, the endless sky, the vast and sometimes empty beaches? Drive thousands of kilometres and still be in the same country? Or call a whole continent your home country? When I look at the risks, the challenges, the thrills I have encountered over the decades, I can most definitely say that coming here has been the biggest adventure of my life.

I have never experienced discrimination as a newcomer, a New Australian, neither at work nor privately, not openly anyway. And I did not go looking or listening for it either. Of course it helped enormously that I felt at ease with the language, despite the early difficulties with mumbling blokes. I started learning English in school in Germany at age ten; then, when I was sixteen, I spent a year as an exchange student in the US and became fluent in English. Knowing a country's language, to me, is a first step – no, it is the prerequisite – on the way to feeling at home in that country, to create that all-important feeling of belonging. How can you ever feel at home in a country if you cannot communicate with your fellow citizens? Cannot chat to your neighbour across the fence? Language is of utmost importance. Always. It opens doors – to employment, to participation, to friendship – and it establishes a sense of belonging, of being in the right place.

I was seven years old when my family was uprooted, when we were expelled from our home in one of Germany's eastern provinces. I may have been just a child but I too felt that sense of loss that my parents felt; their sadness was also my sadness and it has stayed with me ever since. Did I feel that I belonged in the village where my family made their new home after the war? Never quite, never totally. So in a way, it was easy to break away, to leave for distant shores. Do I feel that I belong here? Yes, but again, not quite, not totally.

Apart from the language, there are other important things to learn about the new country, even if is just in small doses – its history, its traditions, its values, its way of life. To my fellow newcomers I say, Be open, be curious, inquisitive. Do not hide away, get out of the house. Mix with others, all sorts of others, and not just your own countrymen. See what others do; you might get some new ideas.

Australia is a country of clubs and organisations. Join a choir, a walking club, a sports club, become involved in your children's school. Be bold. Persevere. Don't shut yourself away, and don't shut your children away. Don't do that to them, let them be; let them be little Aussies, if they want to. And don't be afraid: Australians are generally a friendly and welcoming people, although at times they may be a bit unsure of how to deal with us, the newcomers.

When Chris and I took the big step, the decision to migrate, it was for our own sake. But many migrants do not do so simply for themselves, but also for their children; and in many instances mainly for the children. Our own children are certainly and wholeheartedly true blue Aussies, yet they are aware of, and carry within them, their German heritage. Tim once confided to his uncle in Germany that he was forever grateful to his parents for coming to Australia so that he and his brother could grow up under its big blue sky and in its wide open spaces.

And when we, the newcomers, come to live in this new land, we may find that it is not always easy to strike the right balance between our old life, our old and familiar ways, and this new life here. How far does one go in order to integrate and assimilate? Somehow we want to remain true to ourselves and to our very own personal make-up. We certainly do not want to give up everything we once held dear – be it food, dress, customs, traditions, beliefs – we do not want to give up our old self altogether, and by no means should we. But we also want to fit in, we do want to belong. At least, most of us do. And that decision – the extent to which we want to assimilate and integrate – has to be a very personal one.

One thing, however, we should definitely leave behind is old grievances, old troubles from back home. They do not belong here. Coming here is a new start – we should make the most of it.

www.ingramcontent.com/pod-product-compliance
Lightning Source LLC
Chambersburg PA
CBHW070908080526
44589CB00013B/1218